THE
WAY *of* BEAUTY

THE
WAY *of* BEAUTY

FIVE
MEDITATIONS
FOR
SPIRITUAL
TRANSFORMATION

FRANÇOIS CHENG

TRANSLATED BY JODY GLADDING

Inner Traditions
Rochester, Vermont • Toronto, Canada

Inner Traditions
One Park Street
Rochester, Vermont 05767
www.InnerTraditions.com

Copyright © 2006 by Éditions Albin Michel S.A.
English translation copyright © 2009 by Inner Traditions International

Originally published in French under the title *Cinq méditations sur la beauté* by Éditions Albin Michel S.A.
First U.S. edition published in 2009 by Inner Traditions

Library of Congress Cataloging-in-Publication Data

Cheng, François, 1929–
 [Cinq méditations sur la beauté. English]
 The way of beauty : five meditations for spiritual transformation / François Cheng ; translated by Jody Gladding. — 1st U.S. ed.
  p. cm.
 Includes bibliographical references.
 Summary: "Five meditations on the role of beauty in human life and its direct connection with the sacred"—Provided by publisher.
 ISBN 978-1-59477-287-0
 1. Spirituality in literature. 2. Aesthetics. I. Title.
 PQ2663.H3913C5613 2006
 844.914—dc22

2009017673

Printed and bound in the United States by Lake Book Manufacturing

10 9 8 7 6 5 4 3 2 1

Text design and layout by Virginia Scott Bowman
This book was typeset in Garamond Premier Pro

CONTENTS

INTRODUCTION

FEW BOOKS COME INTO being the way that this one has. The following pages are the fruit of a singular history, a history of encounters. Of course, they also have their prehistory, which is rooted in a life entirely devoted to writing, to the transmission of a thousand-year-old artistic tradition, to the dialogue between Eastern and Western thought. But when François Cheng was on the point of committing the essence of his research and reflections to a small amount of space, as had been his desire for many years, he found himself at a loss.

What he had to say, in the end, went beyond the framework of erudition alone, involved his own personal development at the deepest levels, and could not be summarized in a treatise, which may have been useful, certainly, but not productive. Why speak of beauty if not to attempt to restore man to his best self, and especially to risk speech that can transform him? It was then as if, at the heart of François Cheng, the poet challenged the writer and the scholar; he showed them the indecency of scholarly discourse on a subject where nothing less than human salvation is at stake. He charged them not to evoke the word *beauty* without an acute awareness of the world's barbarity. He proclaimed to them that, faced with the almost universal reign of cynicism, aesthetics can only achieve its true depths by letting itself be subverted by ethics.

Thus it was necessary to return to the essential, that is, to the crucial reality of the "between," to the relationship that unites beings, to "what arises between the living, made up of the unexpected and unhoped-for," of which the poet had already spoken in his introduction to the *Livre du Vide médian*. And thus arose the idea of taking a detour in the writing process, through actual encounters with real people—individuals capable of discernment. Convinced that true beauty unfolds through intersection and interpenetration, François Cheng wanted to appeal to *people,* before whom beauty's words could, almost irresistibly, spill forth. That was how it came about that an informal circle of friends—artists and scientists, philosophers and psychoanalysts, writers and anthropologists, experts or not on the East and China—shared the privilege, over five unforgettable evenings, of witnessing the genesis of these meditations.* Or rather, of sharing the experience of that genesis, so great was the poet's concern with participating in a relationship of creative exchange.

These five meditations thus bear the mark of oral tradition and they must be read accordingly. They often proceed by means of a gradual deepening, taking the form of spiraling thought in which some—inevitable—repetitions are in fact refreshed by the poet's and interlocuters' exchanges. Each participant in these encounters experienced something unusual in these moments of intense presence: a man was entirely devoting himself, with humility, to evoking an apparently "useless" reality, neglected, even ridiculed, by our society. But at the heart of that precious fragility, *between* beings, something unique occurred that each person, in a flash, perceived as fundamental. Born of sharing, these meditations are offered here to be shared with a greater number, so that the spark of beauty they lit can live on.

JEAN MOUTAPPA, DIRECTOR OF THE SPIRITUALITY
DIVISION AT ÉDITIONS ALBIN MICHEL

---

*The author and editor express their gratitude to Ysé Tardan-Masquelier and Patrick Tomatis, who made available a beautiful meditation room at the Center for the Fédération Nationale des Enseignants de Yoga, a very appropriate environment for these sessions.

FIRST MEDITATION

IN THESE TIMES OF universal suffering, random violence, and natural and ecological disasters, to speak of beauty could seem incongruous, improper, even provocative—almost scandalous. But that is precisely why we can see that beauty, as evil's opposite, really is situated at the other extreme of the reality we must face. I am convinced that it is our urgent and ongoing task to take a hard look at these two mysteries, which constitute the two poles of the living universe: at one end, evil; at the other, beauty.

We know what evil is, especially the evil that men inflict upon their fellows. Because of their intelligence and their freedom, when men descend into hatred and cruelty, they can sink to bottomless depths, which not even the most ferocious animal manages to do. Therein lies a mystery that haunts our consciousness, creating a wound that seems never to heal.

We also know what beauty is. Nevertheless, simply reflecting on it is enough to fill us with wonder: the universe is not obliged to be beautiful, and yet it *is* beautiful. In light of this observation, the beauty of the world, despite all the calamities, also appears to us as an enigma.

What does the existence of beauty mean for our own existence? And in the face of evil, what does Dostoyevsky's claim, "Beauty will save the world," mean?[1] Evil and beauty: those are the two challenges we must accept. Nor can the fact escape us that evil and beauty are not just polar opposites; sometimes they are intertwined. Because it is only at the very end of its axis that beauty cannot be turned by evil into an instrument of deceit, domination, or death. When no longer founded on goodness, is beauty still "beautiful"? Wouldn't true beauty itself be a good? Intuitively, we know that to distinguish true beauty from false is part of our task. What is at stake is nothing less than the truth of human destiny, a destiny that implicates the fundamental facts of our freedom.

Perhaps it is worthwhile for me to pause here to offer my own personal reason for wanting to address the question of beauty and not ignore the question of evil. It is because very early on, when I was still a child, I was literally "floored" by these two extreme phenomena. Beauty came first.

I am originally from the Jiangxi Province where Lu Mountain is located; my parents took us to the mountain to stay each summer. Forming part of a mountain chain, Lu Mountain rises to a height of more than two thousand meters, towering over the Yangtze River on one side and Boyang Lake on the other.

Because of its exceptional setting, it is considered one of the most beautiful spots in China. Thus, for some fifteen centuries, it has been beset by hermits, monks, poets, and painters. Discovered by Westerners, Protestant missionaries in particular, toward the end of the nineteenth century it became their vacation place. They congregated around a central hill, dotting it with chalets and cottages. Despite ancient ruins and modern dwellings, Lu Mountain continues to exert its power to fascinate. The surrounding mountains retain their original beauty, a beauty that tradition characterizes as mysterious to the point that the Chinese expression, "the beauty of Lu Mountain" means "an endless mystery."

I am not going to describe that beauty at great lengths. Let me say briefly that it stems from its exceptional setting, as I just mentioned, which offers ever-new perspectives and an infinite play of light. It also stems from the presence of mist and clouds that in turn hide and reveal the mountain face; of fantastic rocks and dense, varied vegetation; of waterfalls and cascades that fill the ear with an uninterrupted music over the course of days and seasons. On summer nights inflamed by fireflies, between the river and the Milky Way, the mountain exhales its scents derived from all the essences; drunk, the aroused beasts give themselves over to the moonlight, the snakes unfurl their satin, the frogs strew their pearls, between two cries, the birds launch jet black arrows. . . .

But my purpose is not descriptive. I wish simply to say that through Lu Mountain, Nature, in all its formidable presence, revealed itself to the child of six or seven that I was then, as an inexhaustible harbor, and above all, as an irrepressible passion. It seemed to call me to participate in its adventure, and that appeal overwhelmed me, left me thunderstruck. Young as I was, I was not unaware that Nature also harbored much violence and cruelty. Nevertheless, how could I not hear the message that resounded within me: beauty exists!

Again within this almost original world, that message would soon be confirmed by the beauty of the human body, or more precisely, the female body. Wandering the footpaths, I would come across young Western women in bathing suits, off for their swim in pools formed by the waterfalls. The bathing suits of that era were modesty itself. But the sight of bare shoulders and bare legs in the summer sun—what a shock! To say nothing of the delighted laughter of those young women responding to the murmur of the waterfalls! It seemed that here Nature had found a specific language, capable of celebrating it. Celebrating—that was the key. It was so essential for humans to make something of this beauty that Nature offered them.

I was soon to discover that magic thing that is art. Wide-eyed, I began to look more attentively at Chinese painting, which so marvelously recreates those misty mountain scenes. And, discovery of discoveries: I soon stumbled upon another kind of painting. One of my aunts, returning from France, brought us reproductions from the Louvre and elsewhere. I had another shock at seeing the nude bodies of women so carnally and ideally displayed: Greek beauties, the models of Botticelli, Titian, and especially, closer to us, Chassériau, Ingres. Emblematic, Ingres's *La Source* penetrated the child's imagination, drew tears from him, stirred his blood.

This was the end of 1936. Less than a year later, the Sino-Japanese War broke out. The Japanese invaders counted on a short war. The Chinese resistance surprised them. When, after several months, they took the capital, the terrible Nanking Massacre took place. I had just turned eight.

In two or three months, the Japanese army, unleashed, succeeded in putting to death three hundred thousand people, using cruel and varied means: they machine-gunned fleeing throngs; they committed mass executions by decapitation—using swords; they threw whole groups of innocent people into wide pits where they were buried alive.

Other scenes of horror: Chinese soldiers taken as prisoners tied upright to posts for Japanese soldiers' bayonet practice. The Japanese soldiers, in a row, faced them. In turn, each soldier stepped out of the line, charged toward his Chinese target, and planted his bayonet in the living flesh. . . .

Just as horrible was the fate reserved for women: individual rape, gang rape often followed by mutilation, by murder. One of the manias of the soldier rapists: photographing the raped woman or women, whom they made stand next to them, nude. Some of those photos were published in Chinese documents denouncing Japanese atrocities. From then on, in the consciousness of the eight-year-old child that I was, superimposed upon the image of ideal beauty in Ingres's *La Source* was that of the violated woman, maimed by her abuser.

Evoking these historical facts, I absolutely do not want to suggest that acts of atrocity are exclusive to a single people. Later would come my time to learn the history of China and the world. I know that evil, that the capacity to do evil, is a universal fact involving the whole of humanity.

These two outstanding, extreme phenomena now continually haunted my awareness. Later it would be easy for me to register that evil and beauty constituted the two extremes of the living universe, that is, reality. Thus I knew that, henceforth, I would have to embrace these two ends: by dealing only with one and neglecting the other, my truth would never be valid. I understood instinctively that without beauty, life was probably not worth the trouble of living, and that, on the other hand, a certain form of evil comes precisely from the horribly perverted use of beauty.

〜

That is why I am coming before you today, very belatedly in my life, to take a hard look at the question of beauty, trying to keep in mind the existence of evil. This is a difficult and thankless task, I know. In this age of confused values, it is deemed better to appear scoffing, cynical, sarcastic, disillusioned, or unconcerned. The courage to confront this task, I believe, stems as much from my desire to fulfill a duty toward those lost and suffering as toward those yet to come.

Nevertheless, how can I not admit that I am full of misgivings, if not seized with anguish? Here before you, I am dreading the questions (even though I find them legitimate), that could arise: "What position are you representing? What is your point of departure? What legitimacy do you lay claim to?" To these questions, I respond quite simply that I have no particular qualifications. A single rule guides me: neglect nothing that is part of life; never refrain from listening to others and thinking for oneself. Undeniably, I come from a certain land and a certain culture. Knowing that culture best, I make it my task to present the best part of it. But the fact of my exile has made me a man from nowhere, or from everywhere.* Thus I do not speak in

---

*François Cheng was born in China in 1929. He went to France in 1948 on a study grant and became a French citizen in 1973. In 2002 he was elected to *L'Académie Française*, the first person of Asian origin to achieve this honor.

the name of a tradition, an ideal handed down from the ancients whose list might be closed, and even less from an already declared metaphysics, or preestablished belief.

I present myself instead as a slightly naive phenomenologist who is observing and interrogating not only the facts already discovered and defined by reason, but also that which is concealed and implied, which arises in unforeseen, unexpected ways, which emerges as gift and promise. I am aware that, within the material order, one can and must establish theorems. But on the other hand I know that within the order of life, it is good to learn to seize phenomena as they occur, each time singular, when they reveal themselves to be following the Way, that is to say, moving toward open life. Beyond my reflections, the work I must accomplish consists rather of hollowing out in myself the capacity for receptivity. Only a posture of welcome—to be the ravine of the world, according to Lao-tzu—and not of conquest, will permit us, I am persuaded, to gather from open life a share of truth.

Pronouncing this word, *truth,* a question comes to mind: I propose to reflect on beauty, very well. Is it therefore legitimate to present it as the supreme manifestation of the created universe? If we look to the Platonic tradition for support, is it not the true—or truth—that must occupy the highest place? And immediately following truth, must that distinction not go to the good or goodness? This very legitimate line of questioning must indeed accompany us throughout our reflections. In developing our ideas on beauty, we must try to justify them, as we proceed, in relationship to notions of truth and goodness.

For the moment, let us begin by advancing the former. That the true, or truth, is fundamental seems evident to us. Since the living universe exists, a truth must exist for such a reality, in its totality, to be able to function. As to the good, or goodness, we also understand its necessity. For this living universe to continue to exist, to endure, there must be a minimum of goodness, or else we would risk killing one another to the very last being, and all would be in vain. And beauty? It exists, without its existence seeming, at first glance, the least bit necessary. It is there in an omnipresent way, insistent, penetrating, all the while giving the impression of being superfluous. That is its mystery: there it is, before our eyes, the greatest mystery.

We could imagine a universe that would only be *true,* never touched by the slightest idea of beauty. This would be a singularly functional universe in which uniform, undifferentiated elements would be dispersed, moving in an absolutely interchangeable fashion. We would be dealing with an order of robots and not one of life. In fact, the concentration camps of the twentieth century provided us with a monstrous image of this "order."

For life to exist, there must be a differentiation of elements. As it evolves, as it becomes increasingly complex, this differentiation results in the singularity of each being. That conforms to the law of life, which implies precisely that each being forms a specific organic unity and possesses at the same time the potential for growth and transformation. That is why the immense adventure of life has resulted in each blade of grass, each flower, each of us, every one, unique and irreplaceable.

This fact is so obvious that it no longer astonishes us, or moves us. Yet, personally, I remain one who has always been astonished by it. In growing older, far from feeling disenchanted, I am still astonished by it. And why not say it: it never ceases to make me glad, because I know that the uniqueness of beings, of each being, represents an extraordinary gift.

I sometimes imagine things slightly differently, telling myself that the differentiation of the elements could have been achieved through large categories. That there might be, for example, the flower category, but with all the flowers alike, or the bird category, but with all the birds identical, the man category, the woman category, and so on.

But no, there is *this* flower, *this* bird, *this* man, *this* woman. Thus for the material order, on the level of function, we can establish theorems; for the order of life, all unity is always unique. We must add here that if each being is unique, it is to the extent that all others also are unique. If I were the only unique being, and if all the others were identical, I would be nothing more than a bizarre specimen, good for displaying in a museum case. The uniqueness of each individual can only be constituted, affirmed, gradually revealed, and finally can only become meaningful in the face of other unique beings, thanks to other unique beings. That is the very condition of open life. It is very much on this condition that an open life does not risk closing down into a deadening narcissism. All true uniqueness solicits other uniquenesses, it only aspires to other uniquenesses.

The fact of uniqueness is verified as much in space as in time. In space, beings notice one another and distinguish one another by their uniqueness. In time, each episode, each experience of each being, is equally stamped with the seal of uniqueness. The idea of these unique moments, when they are happy and beautiful, prompts in us poignant feelings accompanied by infinite longing. We bow before the evidence that the uniqueness of each moment is tied to our condition as mortal beings; it is a continual reminder for us. It is the reason why beauty seems to us nearly always tragic, haunted as we are by the awareness that all beauty is ephemeral. It also provides for us the opportunity to stress here and now that all beauty collaborates precisely with the uniqueness of the moment. True beauty could not be a perpetually fixed state. Its occurrence, its appearance, always constitutes a unique moment; that is its mode of existence. Given that each being is unique, each of its moments is unique, its beauty resides in its momentary surge toward beauty, endlessly renewed, and each time new.

As I see it, uniqueness is precisely where the possibility for beauty begins: the being is no longer a robot among robots, nor simply a figure amid other figures. Uniqueness transforms each being into presence, which, in the image of a flower or a tree, never ceases to open, in time, toward the plenitude of its radiance, which is the very definition of beauty.

As presence, each being is virtually inhabited by the capacity for beauty, and especially by the "desire for beauty." At first glance, the universe is populated only by a set of figures; in reality, it is populated by a set of presences. I almost think that each presence, which cannot be reduced to anything else, proves to be a transcendence. With regard more specifically to the human figure, I like and embrace this idea of Henri Maldiney's

> From each human face radiates an unpossessable transcendence that envelops us and traverses us. This transcendence is not that of a particular psychological expression, but that which each face's quality of being, its metaphysical dimension, requires. It is the transcendence of reality questioning itself in it, reflecting in it, and in that very questioning the exclamatory dimension of the Open.[2]

It is from this reality that the possibility of saying "I" and "you" is born, that the possibility of language is born, and perhaps also, the possibility of love.

But to stay with our theme of beauty, we can observe that within the presence of each being, and from presence to presence, a complex network of circulation and interconnection is established. Precisely within this network is located the desire each being feels to open toward the plenitude of its presence in the world. The more conscious a being is, the more complex this desire grows: desire for self, desire for the other, desire for transformation in the sense of a transfiguration. And in a more secret, more mystical way, another desire—the desire to reunite with the original Desire from which the universe itself seems to proceed, to the extent that this universe appears in its entirety as a presence full of manifest or hidden splendor. In this context, the transcendence of each being of whom we have just spoken is only revealed, can only exist, in a relationship that heightens it and extends beyond it. True transcendence, paradoxically, is located in the *between,* in that which bursts forth most intensely when decisive exchange between beings and Being takes place.

SECOND MEDITATION

DURING OUR LAST MEDITATION, I said that, by transforming beings into presence, uniqueness makes beauty possible. That does not prevent us from asking that nagging question once again: the universe is not obliged to be beautiful, but it is beautiful; can we find meaning in this? Is beauty only superfluous, something extra, a decorative addition, a kind of "cherry on the cake"? Or do its roots go deeper, does it obey some intentionality of a more ontological nature?

⸋

That we find the magnificence of the universe striking, that Nature reveals itself to be fundamentally beautiful: these are facts confirmed by our universally shared experience. Let us be careful not to forget the beauty of the human face: the face of women celebrated by the Renaissance painters; the face of men delineated by certain icons. Limiting ourselves to Nature alone, it is not difficult to distinguish a few of the elements that comprise the feeling of beauty we all experience:

- the midnight blue splendor of a starry sky
- the magnificence of the sunrise and sunset everywhere in the world
- the majesty of a great river surging through rocky narrows and nurturing fertile plains
- the mountain rising high with its snow-covered summit, its verdant slopes and flowering valleys
- an oasis blooming in the heart of a desert
- a cypress standing in the middle of a field
- the superb flight of antelope across the savannah
- a flock of wild birds soaring over a lake

All these scenes are so well known that they have almost become clichés. Our capacity to feel astonishment and wonder at them is diminished, whereas each scene, each time unique, ought to provide us the opportunity for seeing the universe as if for the first time, at the dawn of the world.

Here, already, a question arises for us. This natural beauty that we observe—is it a fundamental quality, intrinsic to the self-generating universe, or does it result from accident, chance? The question is legitimate since, according to some theories, life is simply the result of the fortuitous encounter of various chemical elements. By these accounts, something began to move and that is how matter came to life. Some theories happily depict life as an epiphenomenon, and to make it more colorful, as a "mold" on the surface of a planet, which itself is lost like a grain of sand in a vast ocean of galaxies. Nevertheless, this mold began to function, to become increasingly complex to the point of producing the imagination and the mind. Not content with merely functioning, it succeeded in perpetuating itself by establishing the laws of transmission. Not content with merely transmitting itself, it set about becoming beautiful.

That the mold began to function by evolving is astonishing. That it succeeded in enduring through self-transmission is even more astonishing. That it tends, one could almost say irrepressibly, toward beauty, is absolutely astounding! Thus one beautiful day, by the luck of the draw, matter became beautiful. Unless, from the first, matter had potentially contained a promise of beauty, a capacity for beauty?

We will not seek vainly to decide between a "cynical" and a more "inspiring" theory. The important thing for us is to remain faithful to reality, to all of reality, to be humble enough to welcome all the facts that call out to us, that will not leave us alone.

We can objectively observe that, in fact, our sense of the sacred, of the divine, does not come from simply witnessing the truth, that is to say, something that carries out its function, that operates smoothly. It comes much more from witnessing beauty, that is, something that is striking for its enigmatic splendor, that dazzles and enthralls. The universe no longer appears as a given; it reveals itself to be a gift, inviting gratitude and celebration. In his work *La Parole et la Beauté*, Alain Michel, emeritus professor at the Sorbonne, asserts, "As all ancient Greek philosophers believed, the sacred appears bound to the beautiful."[1] All the great religious texts take the same position. Without needing to consult them, we can observe this ourselves. Is it not the presence of a very high mountain perpetually crowned with snow—which Kant classes among the sublime entities—that inspires the sacred veneration of area inhabitants? Is it not at the most awe-filled moments, the moments approaching ecstasy, that we exclaim to ourselves, "How divine!"

If I continue to follow this line of thought, I would say that our sense of sense, our sense of a universe possessing sense, also comes from beauty. This is true precisely to the extent that this universe, composed of palpable and perceptible elements, always adopts a precise orientation, tending like a flower or a tree toward the realization of the desire for the full radiance of being it bears within itself, to the point of manifesting the plenitude of its presence in the world.

Within this process, we can find the three meanings of the French word *sens:* sensation, direction, and signification.

It is an understatement to say that man has a relationship with beauty. In the midst of the tragic human condition, it is, in fact, from beauty that we draw meaning and pleasure. Moreover, as we approach the question of artistic creation, we will try to refer to a few great aesthetic traditions, and to distinguish certain criteria for gauging and judging beauty. For the moment, suffice it to say that the beauty I have witnessed is not limited to combinations of external traits, to appearances, which can be described using a whole arsenal of qualifiers: pretty, attractive, colorful, sparkling, sumptuous, elegant, harmonious, well-proportioned, and so on.

Formal beauty exists, of course, but it hardly encompasses the entire reality of beauty. That is more strictly a matter of Being, moved by the imperious desire for beauty. True beauty does not reside only in what is already manifest as beauty; it resides almost primarily in the desire and the impulse. It is a *becoming,* and the dimension of spirit or soul is vital to it. Accordingly, it is governed by the principle of life. Thus, beyond all the possible criteria, only one thing guarantees its authenticity: true beauty is that which follows the course of the Way, the irresistible progress toward open life—in other words, a principle of life that keeps its whole promise open. This criterion based on the principle of life—and I have not forgotten the question of death, which we will come to— excludes all use of beauty as a tool of deception or domination. Such use is ugliness itself; it always constitutes a path of destruction. Yes, we must always avoid confusing the essence of a thing and the uses to which it can be put. How true that is with regard to beauty!

To further clarify my remarks, again, let me add this: beauty is something that is virtually there, eternally there. It is a desire that bursts forth from within beings, or Being, like an inexhaustible fountain that, more than an isolated, anonymous form, reveals itself as radiant, connected presence, inspiring acquiescence, interaction, and transfiguration.

A matter of being and not of having, true beauty cannot be defined as a means or instrument. In essence, it is a way to be, a state of existence. Let us observe this through one of the symbols of beauty: the rose. We risk falling into "rosy" discourse! Let us run that risk. By what course of habit and distortion has the rose become a somewhat banal, slightly mawkish image, even while the universe had to evolve over billions of years in order to produce this miraculous entity of harmony, coherence, and resolution? Let us agree to take a good, long look at the rose. Let us begin by recalling this couplet by the seventeenth-century Silesian poet Angelus Silesius, who is associated with Flemish-Rhenish mystics like Meister Eckhart and Jakob Böhme:

> The rose is without a why, flowers because it
>   flowers;
> Without concern for itself, or desire to be seen.[2]

Well-known, admirable lines before which one can only bow. Indeed, the rose is without a why, as are all living beings, all of us. If a naive observer wanted to add something nevertheless, he could say this: to be fully a rose, in its uniqueness, and nothing else at all—that constitutes sufficient reason to be. That requires the rose to bring into play all the vital energy at its disposal. From the moment its shoot emerges from the earth, it pushes in one direction, as if driven by an unwavering will. Through it, a line of force is established that is crystallized in a bud. Beginning from this bud, the leaves and then the petals will soon form and open out, adopting such curvature, such sinuousness, opting for such fragrance, such a hue. Henceforth, nothing will prevent it from completing its signature, fulfilling its desire to be fulfilled, to be nourished by the soil, but also by the wind, the dew, the rays of the sun. All of this is done with a view toward the plenitude of its being, a plenitude already present in its seed, at the very distant origin of all eternity, we might say.

And finally there it is, the rose, manifested in the full radiance of its presence, propagating its rhythmic waves toward its aspiration: pure, limitless space. This irrepressible opening into space evokes a fountain endlessly pouring forth from the depths. Because insofar as the rose desires to last for the time of its destiny, it also depends on being deeply rooted. Between the soil and the air, between earth and sky, a give and take occurs. This is symbolized by the very form of the petals, a form so specific, simultaneously curved inward and turning outward in a gesture of offering. Jacques de Bourbon Busset summarizes it in a lovely phrase: "brightness of the flesh, shadow of the spirit." Indeed, it is fitting that the flesh be in the light, the spirit in shadow, in order for the latter to support the principle of life that governs the flesh, so that even when the petals have fallen and mixed with the nurturing humus, their invisible perfume may persist as an emanation of their essence or a sign of their transfiguration.

"In a gesture of offering," we said. Nevertheless, the poet wrote, "without concern for itself, or desire to be seen." It is true that since the why of a rose is to be fully a rose, the moment of its plenitude of being coincides with the plenitude of Being itself. In other words, the desire for beauty is absorbed into the beauty; it no longer has to justify itself. If we want to continue thinking in terms of "being seen" and "not being seen," we can say that—beyond the role it plays in "educating" the human gaze—the rose's beauty, its radiance resonating with the full radiance of the universe, can finally only be taken in by the divine gaze. By which I mean: gathered in, not gathered!

This recalls to mind what I said about the three meanings of the word *sens*. Indeed, this monosyllabic word seems to consolidate or contain within it the three essential states of Being as enumerated by the rose: sensation, direction, signification. Let us make it clear that by signification, we do not necessarily mean an intentional act with a view toward something. If there is a goal, it is pleasure, insofar as it is true that we can only fully enjoy Being by delighting in all our senses. These senses include that instinctive knowledge of our own presence in the world as a "sign of life," a sign that calls into play all the potentialities and possibilities we bear within ourselves.

Sensation should not be limited to its sensorial level, and beauty is very much that potentiality and possibility toward which every being tends. Here, again almost inevitably, we slide from the French word *sens* to a Chinese character that is its equivalent, if not a richer version of it, the character *yi* 意.

⌒◦⌒

Fundamentally, the ideogram *yi* designates what comes from the depths of a being: radiance, desire, intention, inclination. All of these meanings can be encompassed approximately into the idea of "intentionality." Combined with other characters, it provides a series of composite words with various meanings but organically linked to one another. They can be roughly organized into two categories: those that involve mind—idea, consciousness, intention, will, orientation, signification; and those belonging to soul—charm, taste, desire, feeling, aspiration, spirit. Finally, overarching them all is the expression *yi-jing*, "superior state of the mind, supreme dimension of the soul."

This last concept, *yi-jing*, merits further attention. In China, it became the most important criterion for judging the value of a poetic or pictorial work. We will come back to this. According to its definition, we can see that it dealt just as much with mind as with soul: the mind and soul of the artist who created the work, of course, but also the mind and soul of the living universe, a universe that makes itself, that creates itself, as Chinese designates by the term *Zao-wu*, "Creation," indeed even *Zao-wu-zhe*, "Creator." In a general way, it is often said that Chinese thought does not include the idea of Creation in the biblical sense of the word. It is true that Chinese thought has not been possessed by the idea of a personal God; on the other hand, it does manifestly include the sense of origin and engendering, as Lao-tzu's assertions demonstrate: "What is comes from what is not"; "the original Tao engenders the One, the One engenders the Two, the Two engenders the Three, the Three engenders the Ten Thousand beings."[3] That certainly comes close to the concept of the demiurge, even while containing more complexity, more subtlety.

After Zhuangzi—one of Taoism's founding fathers from the fourth century BCE—who used this word *Zao-wu-zhe,* "Creator," on two occasions, poets and thinkers throughout history—Liu Zongyuan, Su Shi, Li Qingzhao, Zhu Xi, and Zheng Xie, for example—developed the idea of *Zao-wu-you-yi:* "Creator or Creation is endowed with desire, intention." So much so that the great eighteenth-century theologian Bu Yantu was able to affirm succinctly that "The power of *yi* is most certainly immense; it presided over Heaven and Earth."

I mention these ideas to convey that, according to the Chinese perspective, a creative work, an individual's created work or the living universe as a created work, proceeds certainly from form, but to what a great extent from *yi* as well! It is to the extent that *yi* attains its highest expression in a particular work, to the point of resonating in harmony with the universal *yi,* that the work acquires its value in terms of plenitude and beauty. Beyond its meaning as "superior state of the mind, supreme dimension of the soul," the *yi-jing* in question thus signifies "harmony, sympathy, accord."

From a Chinese perspective, the beauty of a thing thus resides in its *yi,* that invisible essence that drives it. The *yi* is

its eternal flavor, which endlessly produces its scent and resonance. When speaking of a person whose soul does not die
and whose presence endures, one uses the expression *lui-fang-
bai-shi,* which means, "his scent that remains is imperishable."
Here, the scent that conjoins body and soul becomes the sign
of the soul itself. Thus, to come back to the rose, it is through
its scent that it attains the infinity of its being. Scent is no
longer just an accessory for the rose; it is essential to it, in the
sense that its scent allows it to return to the continuous Way,
which opens into the invisible.

Moreover, the Chinese imagination conceives of scent
and resonance as the two preeminent attributes of the invisible, both proceeding, as we have said, from rhythmic waves.
They are combined, for example, in the expression, "scent of
the flowers and song of the birds," to evoke an idyllic scene,
and in the expression, "the scent of incense and the sound
of a gong," to evoke a religious atmosphere or spiritual state.
But most importantly, these two attributes are combined to
form a single ideogram, *xin* 馨, which means precisely, "scent
that spreads far; imperishable scent."

This ideogram is composed of two parts. For the upper
part, it uses the sign 殷, "musical stone," and for the lower part,
the sign 香, "scent." It recalls the "Gan-ying" ("Resonance")
chapter of the Huainanzi, an early Han Taoist treatise from
the second century BCE: in high antiquity, when a god struck
the musical stone, a resonance was produced that emanated
from stone to stone into the far distance, without ever dis-
appearing. The entire ideogram confirms this: rather than a
fleeting fragrance, the scent is a lasting song.

Nearly all Western poets have celebrated flowers, and many of them have celebrated the rose. I could cite Ronsard, Marceline Desbordes-Valmore, and especially Rilke. But let us listen to Claudel, for the simple reason that I am in the process of reading him, on the occasion of the fiftieth anniversary of his death. Let us listen first to this passage in which, by the light of the Tao, that is to say, the "Way of open life," he speaks of living things that take seed in the darkness of Creation's soil, much as we have just described the rose's irresistible desire for growth. In *Connaissance de l'Est,* he says:

> What is the Tao? . . . Below all forms, what has no form, what sees without eyes, what guides without knowledge, ignorance that is the supreme knowledge. Would it be wrong to call this sap the *Mother,* this secret flavor of things, this taste of *Cause,* this shiver of authenticity, this milk that instructs from the *Source*? Ah, we are in the midst of nature like a litter of wild boars who suckle a dead sow! What does Laozi tell us if not to close our eyes and put our mouths to the very source of Creation?[4]

Let us now listen to this passage from the "Cantique de la Rose."

> The rose, what is the rose? Oh rose! What! When we breathe in that odor that brings the gods to life, we only

come to this little insubstantial heart that, as soon as we seize it between our fingers, loses it petals and melts, like flesh from itself, all in its own kiss, a thousand times pursed and folded? Ah, I tell you, that is not the whole rose at all! It is its odor once inhaled that is eternal! Not the scent of the rose alone! It is the scent of everything God made in his summer! No rose, but this perfect speech in ineffable circumstances, in which everything, finally for a moment at this supreme hour, is born! Oh paradise in the shadows! It is reality that dawns for an instant for us under these fragile veils, and the soul's profound delight at all things God has made! For a perishable being, what is more fatal to exhale than this eternal essence, and for a second, the inexhaustible odor of the rose? The more a thing dies, the more it arrives at its end, the more it expires from this word that it cannot say and from this secret that draws it! Ah, that at the middle of the year, this instant of eternity is fragile, but extreme and suspended![5]

Claudel locates the rose in the context of the time, more precisely in the moment of eternity. He emphasizes the rose's scent, which is ephemeral and "inexhaustible" at the same time. No doubt the poet was not unaware of the scientific explanation of the scent's usefulness. But he is filled with wonder that such an essence can exist. The scent is experienced as the invisible part of the rose, its superior part, the part that is its soul, so to speak. The scent is not limited by form, nor by a restricted space. It is in some way the transmutation of the rose into wave, into song, into the realm of the infinite.

In saying that, I immediately recall the line from Baudelaire, "Happy is the one who soars over life, and understands without effort the language of flowers and mute things."[6] Indeed, for the one who knows how to receive it, or hear it, this scent incites an almost unspeakable rapture; it endures in the receiver's memory as something more ethereal, more quintessential, and more durable. Even as the petals fade and fall to the ground, the scent hovers there in the memory, a reminder that those petals, mixed with the humus, will be reborn in the form of another rose, that, from the visible to the invisible and from the invisible to the visible, the order of life continues by way of universal transformation.

⌒ ⌒

Following Claudel's presentation of the rose as the incarnation of the eternal moment, I would like to expand upon this idea and approach the question of the relationship that beauty maintains with time in general and, implicitly, with death. Let us say first of all that the opposite of the order of life is not natural death, which, precisely as a natural phenomenon, is an integral part of life. For life to be life, which implies growth and renewal, death must be an inevitable, if not a necessary, constituent. And in the process of time, as we have said, it is the perspective of death that renders each and every moment unique. Death contributes to the uniqueness of life. If there is evil, it lies in abnormal, tragic occurrences and in those corrupted, perverted uses of death. These last, especially, are located outside the order of life; they are capable of destroying the order of life itself.

In short, it is useful to distinguish two kinds of deaths, which, moreover, is what Lao-tzu, the founder of Taoism, did. This thinker about the Way—the progression of the order of life—asserted in a prophetic phrase: "To die without perishing, that is long life."[7] Both the character *si*, "to die," and the character *wang*, "to perish," mean "cessation of life," according to standard usage. But from Lao-tzu's perspective, the character *si* takes on the meaning of "returning to the Way."

What is "long life"? Undeniably, the human mind dreams of eternity. It aspires to an eternity of beauty, of course, and not of unhappiness, all the while knowing that all beauty is nevertheless fragile, and thus ephemeral. Have we not just come upon a contradiction? Perhaps the answer depends on the way we conceive of eternity. Would eternity be the flat repetition of itself? In which case, it would not be a matter of true beauty, or of true life. Because, let us repeat, true beauty is the impulse of Being toward beauty, and the renewal of that impulse; true life is the impulse of Being toward life and the renewal of that impulse. A good eternity could only be made up of salient moments in which life bursts forth toward its full ecstatic intensity.

If that is true, we have the impression of knowing a bit of this eternity, since our human life span is substantially the same. It also consists of salient moments when life leaps toward the Open, does it not? In that case, we are already part of eternity, we are in eternity! Some may find this vision far too angelic. Then let us reserve it for those naive souls among us!

In the meantime, what is important to us is our human life span. I use the term *durée,* duration, rather than *temps,* time, on purpose here. Whereas *time* evokes a mechanical flow, an implacable series of lapses and losses, *duration* alludes to a qualitative continuity in which those things experienced and dreamed of form an organic present. I borrow this term *durée,* duration, from Bergson, of course. By simplifying to the extreme, at the risk of distorting it, let us attempt to summarize that philosopher's thinking as follows.

If, outwardly, each of us suffers the tyranny of the flow of time, within each individual consciousness, thanks to memory, our experiences and imaginings, but also the elements that make up our knowledge, constitute an organic duration that transcends, so to speak, the breaks, gaps, and separations in time and space. The components of this duration remain in a "contemporaneousness" that makes light of the chronology and converges continually toward a present: a present that, in fact, continually opens onto a past and into a future. That occurs in the image of a melody, which is not formed by a simple addition of notes and in which each note follows from the preceding one and colors the following one. Duration operates within itself as well. Through a continuous process, each component allows itself to be marked by the others, all the while leaving its mark on the others.

If we return to the theme of beauty, we can say that in the duration that inhabits a consciousness, beauty attracts beauty, in the sense that an experience of beauty recalls other previous experiences of beauty, and, at the same time, it calls to future experiences of beauty. The more intense the experience of beauty, the more the poignant nature of its brevity creates the desire to renew the experience, inevitably in a different form, since every experience is unique. In other words, within the consciousness in question, where nostalgia and hope merge, each experience of beauty recalls a paradise lost and appeals to a paradise promised.

It is probably in this light that we must understand the line by the poet John Keats: "A thing of beauty is a joy for ever."[8] This is because we become aware that beauty can be a lasting gift, if we recall that it is a promise kept from the beginning. That is why the desire for beauty is no longer limited to an object of beauty; it aspires to rejoining the original desire for beauty that presided at the advent of the universe, the adventure of life. Each experience of beauty, so brief in time, even as it transcends time, restores to us the freshness of the dawn of the world.

THIRD MEDITATION

UNTIL NOW WE HAVE focused primarily on the beauty that comes from Nature. I have intentionally set aside beauty as related to the human. Not that the human is not part of Nature, but among humans, the question arises in a far more complex way. To greatly oversimplify, I would say that, to me, this complexity comes

first of all from the fact that human beings are constituted
of multiple levels, and that, furthermore, because of a certain
degree of intelligence and freedom that they enjoy, they are
quite capable of using beauty in sophisticated, perverse ways.
Aware of their mortality, driven by urgency, men are often
those wild animals seeking any means by which to satisfy
their most pressing instincts.

Among the multiple levels that constitute the human
being, at least two are universally recognized, that is, the
physical and the mental. The second, governed by the mind,
includes its share of the conscious and the unconscious, the
imaginative and the rational, the psychological and what is
characterized as the spiritual. This last part, the spiritual,
is undoubtedly the most controversial; it can be considered
a level all by itself. And this subject will lead us to speak of
the soul. So many elements and interferences enter into the
human constitution that our ideas with regard to beauty are
among our most confused. Attempting to disentangle true
beauty from false is not at all easy for us, nor is it easy to
formulate criteria that allow us to extricate the real values.

Let us assemble the ideas that we have been able to
formulate thus far: the beauty we have in mind is the one
that falls within the domain of Being, that bursts forth
from within Being as an impulse toward beauty, toward the
plenitude of its presence, in the direction of open life. Thus
we are situating ourselves resolutely beyond all "beauty of
appearance," which depends on the combination of external characteristics alone, or is composed entirely of artifice. This is any beauty that can be used as an instrument

to coerce, deceive, or dominate. This "beauty," which is a matter of *having,* as opposed to being, is ubiquitous in societies devoted to consumption, it is true. Its existence is self-justifying; its pernicious use alters its nature. Finally, we can say that artificial beauty, degraded by its exchange value or its power of conquest, never attains the state of communion and love that, in the final analysis, must be beauty's reason for existing. On the contrary, it always signifies a game of deception, destruction, and death: the "ugliness of the soul" that appearances deprive of any chance to remain "beautiful" and to embark in the direction of open life.

Here, a critical voice makes itself heard, a critical but completely necessary and constructive voice; it obliges me to further clarify my stance and my approach. This is the gist of what this critical voice says to me: "You speak of beauty made of appearances and artifice, but in Nature, all beauty is a lure. If some flower or another opens its petals and emits its fragrance, it is to attract the insects that it devours. If the butterfly has colored patterned wings, it is to camouflage itself or distinguish itself sexually. If the peacock fans its tail feathers, it is to entice the female."

To which I respond: these "self-interested" examples of beauty demonstrate at least that beauty possesses the gift of prompting desire and pursuit. As for the examples of beauty I cited to illustrate the beauty of Nature, they are not self-interested, the high mountain crowned in mist, the spring that bursts forth and expands to become a river . . .

The critical voice stops me: "The mountain that you loved so much was originally only an accident in the landscape caused by movements in the earth's surface. The Himalayas which you say inspire sacred veneration resulted from the terrible collision of the drifting continents."

My response to this claim will be more elaborate, at the risk of seeming laborious: "I see things otherwise. As a good Chinese, I believe in the Breath, including the Breath that animates the movements of the earth. And I am grateful to the Breath of that telluric movement for being well inspired, for not leaving the surface of the earth smooth and flat as a board. That would have resulted in a terribly boring monotony, a terrible 'platitude,' which comes from the French word for flat, *plat*. I am grateful to it for having thus given rise to that marvelous thing that is the mountain that elevates life, where the Breaths of the earth and those of the sky can better be exchanged. From within the mountain bursts forth the spring, which, flowing toward the base and expanding, becomes the river. From that moment on, mountain and river are the highest embodiment of the two vital principles, Yang and Yin. The river flows, and nurtures the fertile plains; it symbolizes the flow of time as well, apparently following a straight line and never returning. But only apparently, because true time, in reality, is circular and nonlinear: the river water, even as its flows, evaporates; it rises toward the sky, is transformed into clouds, and falls again as rain on the mountain to renourish the river at its source. Thus, above the 'down-to-earth' one-way flow, this circular movement takes place between earth and sky. The mountain calls out to the sea, the sea responds to the mountain—therein lies the beauty of this law of life. . . ."

Once again the critical voice stops me in my overly lyrical outburst: "That is all very beautiful, but it is a mental construction made by humans after the fact." To that remark let us give the following provisional response: our task cannot be limited to just explaining how matter functions. That is the intention of science. We are intent on life, stretching toward a life always more heightened and more open. Human beings are not outside of everything else, building sand castles on an empty beach. They issue from the adventure of life. Their capacity to stretch toward the mind, their faculty for thought, for developing ideas, are part of the adventure of life. Even while seeming to be completely lost within the universe, we can imagine that we are also the awakened consciousness and beating heart of the material world. The universe thinks of us just as we think of it; we can be the gaze and the speech of the living universe, or at least its interlocutors.

Yes, precious speech. Not only the grammar that allows language to function, but living, creative speech. There is nothing wrong with "theoretical views" as long as they increase our chances of moving in the direction of a higher life. If that is the case, let us welcome them. If that is not the case, let us reject them. To generate them, to judge their value, sincere collective inquiry and true intersubjectivity are of supreme importance. That is the very reason why we are here.

Let us come back to human beings and their various constituent levels. First of all, let us consider the physical level, and say that physical beauty does exist and that, inhabited by desire, it is replete with seduction. Thus, why should we be astonished that it plays its part as lure, encouraged as it is to dazzle or to please? Nevertheless that is the level at which we began, the means by which we acquired and refined our sense of the beautiful, thanks to which we became connoisseurs and appreciators of beauty. But we have expanded and heightened our notion of beauty beyond this basic training. Because formal beauty, as it is manifested in the organization of the human body all the way to the laws governing the movement of celestial bodies, suggests to us an almost ethical beauty, in the sense that it allows constantly maintained requirements to show through, a promise that never fails. And this ethical aspect awakens us to other kinds of beauty, coming from the mind and soul.

But let us remain for the moment with the theme of physical beauty. In this regard, I have seen physical beauty as much in men as in women. Nevertheless, if we are gentlemanly, and especially if we are Chinese, we must grant preeminence to feminine beauty, which, as they say, is the miracle of miracles.

"If we are Chinese," I said. Because the Chinese are worshippers of Nature, and they are fond of metaphors. Through a practice uninterrupted for three thousand years, Chinese poetry literally transformed all the beautiful elements of Nature into metaphors. In these are crystallized all that is sensorial, all that is carnal, in the living universe. If, in the eyes of the Chinese poets, woman appears as a miracle of Nature, it is because they see in her a kind of "concentration" of the beautiful elements of Nature, and because many metaphors can be, quite naturally, applied to her body. Moon, star, breeze, cloud, spring, wave, hill, valley, pearl, jade, flower, fruit, nightingale, dove, gazelle, panther, such curves, such meanderings, such sinuousness, such crevices, so many signs of an endless mystery.

Both Greek and Roman art celebrated the female figure. But it was the Renaissance that literally exploded the Western desire to show the woman in all her carnal radiance: Lippi, Botticelli, Titian, Leonardo da Vinci, Raphael . . .

Let us consider the Mona Lisa, which is universally admired. But first let us briefly digress to mention a decisive stage in the long evolution of the human body. We cannot help but note this: between the Mona Lisa and the cave woman, it is as though there is a "qualitative leap." Nevertheless, the promise of human beauty is already found in the cave woman. Because "standing up" marked the inaugural moment of a distinctly human existence. This upright position led to a three-fold liberation. It freed the hands, which permitted the *homo faber*. It freed the glottis and the vocal cords, which permitted the human voice to become that magical tool for speech and song, allowing the human being to become that creature of language and thought.

And finally, it freed the face; instead of being a muzzle stretched forward close to the ground, as an animal wanders here and there searching for food, the face henceforth was part of the head that rested calmly and nobly on the shoulders. This face could turn with sovereign ease to look toward the heights and the distance, to exchange a smile with its kind, to let surface feelings and emotions that come from the depths and rise to the heights and that eventually shape it. Let us be bold enough to claim that if any hate-filled face is ugly, on the other hand, any human face in its goodness is beautiful. The face is that unique treasure we each offer to the world. And we can speak of the face very much in terms of an offering, or an opening. Because in the final analysis, the mystery and beauty of a face can only be apprehended and revealed through other gazes, or through another light. On this subject, let us admire the beautiful French word for face, *visage*. It suggests a country, *paysage,* that bares or unfurls itself, and thus leads to the idea of a vis-à-vis.

Coming back to the Mona Lisa, her beauty is not only based on the combination of external features; it is also illuminated by a look and a smile, an enigmatic smile that seems to want to say something. How we would love to hear her voice! The voice itself and what the voice says are part of a woman's beauty. Through the voice, a woman expresses her feelings, but also her longings, her dreams, and that unspeakable part that nevertheless tries to be spoken. The desire to speak merges with the desire for beauty; the desire to speak adds to the charm of beauty. This obvious fact thus strikes us: female beauty is not solely the result of physiological evolution; it is also a conquest of the mind. This conquest reveals to us that true beauty is consciousness of beauty and impulse toward beauty, that it inspires love and enriches our conception of love.

In humans, the mind governs the faculty of reason and comprehension, and also imagination and urges. From the mind, we move, without transition, to the soul. We have no choice but to note that, with regard to beauty and love, the idea of the soul runs like a gold thread through the entire span of the Western imagination, from Socrates and Plato, through Plotinus and Saint Augustine, to the classical and Romantic poets.

Let us read Saint Augustine. In his "Sermon on Providence," after having praised that miraculous equilibrium that is the human body, he writes,

> First, let man be constituted with a soul and a body, and let him move by the invisible substance, superior to that which is visible and subject—thus there will be a natural authority, which is the sovereign soul, and a natural obedience, which is the submissive flesh, and therein lies the beauty of a remarkable order. And in the soul itself, let reason (or the mind), through the excellence of its nature, have the highest value and prevail over all its other parts; is not this also an order to be remarked upon? Because no one at this point is the plaything of his desires so that he would hesitate in his response if asked which is worth more, that which is swept along by the unreflective appetites or that which is directed by reason and reflection. From this fact, even someone living without prudence or reason responds despite everything to the question of the best solution, and even if his acts have not corrected him, the question has certainly alerted him. Also, even with a person who behaves in a depraved manner, the voice of order is not silenced when nature brings out his vice.[1]

Now I would like to quote Michelangelo. In a sonnet addressed to the beloved, this is the substance of what he says: "I must love in you that part that you yourself love; it is your soul. To fall in love with your soul, I must not draw from my body alone, but very much from my soul."[2] The soul takes charge of the body, without being hindered by the body, and the soul falls in love with the soul. Its true nature is its capacity to connect with everything; thus its dimension is the infinite. It is very much as soul to soul and not as body to body that total communion can be achieved. Everything occurs as if the physical world would like to train us and initiate us to beauty by demonstrating that beauty *exists,* by signifying to us furthermore that it is extensible and transformable, that beginning with formal beauty, other harmonics, other resonances, other transfigurations are possible.

In the light of the soul, it is good for us to return for a moment to the Mona Lisa, to her look and her smile. Truly there is something mysterious about the look. Where does the beauty of a look come from? Does it reside simply in the physical aspects of the eyes: eyelids, eyelashes, eye color, and so on? The physical beauty of the eyes can certainly contribute to it, to the extent that this beauty is capable of awakening the sense of beauty in the being gratified by it. Now, as we have said, true beauty is precisely the consciousness of beauty and the impulse toward beauty. But because of that very fact, the look is more than the eyes. Don't all languages express the idea that the eyes are the "windows of the soul"? The beauty of a look comes from a light that wells up from the depths of Being. It can also come from an external light that illuminates it, especially when the light captures in an instant something beautiful, or when it encounters another look of love and beauty.

Each of us has already experienced that intense moment when, during an exceptional concert or theater event, all the participants' faces are transfigured, so clearly does beauty attract, increase, and heighten beauty. That is consistent again with what we read in Saint Augustine: according to him, beauty results from the encounter between the interior of a being and the splendor of the cosmos, which, for him, is the sign of the glory of God. This encounter in some way annihilates the separation of the internal and external.

If the beauty of the world forms a landscape, a being's soul is a landscape as well, which Verlaine expresses in the line "Your soul is a chosen landscape . . . ," and which the Chinese aesthetic designates by the term "feeling-landscape."[3] The soul's landscape is made up of memories and dreams, fears and desires, experienced and anticipated scenarios.

Thus let us turn our attention, for the third time, to the Mona Lisa. Shouldn't there be a key to unlock the mystery of her look? Could it possibly be that misty landscape behind her, both distant and near? Here, let us listen to France Quéré who writes in *Le Sel et le Vent:*

In forms of rocks and lakes burst the strange soundings of an interior world. . . . At the height of the [Mona Lisa's] shoulders, an ochre landscape of hilly terrain begins, which the efflorescence of the rocks run through. To the left, the path opens onto the gray waters of a lake, striated by the shadows of the over-hanging rocks. These are thrust faults, manes, fierce necks, deformed muzzles that rise above the waters in a burst of petrified anger. A prehistoric violence blocks the view. . . . To the right, beside the young woman's turned-up mouth, the path follows the course of the muddy river, threading its way up from level to level, among the fallen rocks, finally reaching the shore of a second lake, higher than the first. . . . This is another world, immaterial, immensely contemplative, toward which the smile and the movement of the eyes subtly direct us. A dim glow makes the high altitude lake just barely iridescent. But the maledictions of the shadows and obstructions are vanquished. Other rocks rise, but they no longer shade or enclose anything. Their shadow traces a ring, suggests transparency, leaves the mirror of the waters intact. . . . Between the two purified shores opens a gap where the gold of the water and the light merge, and extend together toward infinity. Is this a god who welcomes the traveler? Is it the joy of an enlightened intelligence at the height of its meditation? . . . Is it childhood rediscovered, made more beautiful by the distances of memory? . . . A human dream begins there, at the height of the eyes and the pure forehead. Its dawns are even more beautiful than the hills of Florence in the sun's first rays.[4]

Taking into account this original landscape, a landscape already containing the promise of beauty, the Mona Lisa no longer appears to us as the simple portrait of a socially prominent woman, but as a miraculous manifestation of that potential beauty the universe promises from the very first. Her smile and look thus become the sign of an intuitive awareness, an awareness of a gift that comes from afar. Most importantly, they signify to us that authentic incarnate beauty is never the beauty of a single isolated face. It is transfiguration, thanks to the encounter of interior light and another light forever offered but so often obscured. *Transfiguration* is understood here as that which is transformed from within, and also as that which shows through in the space of life between the finite and the infinite, between the visible and the invisible.

⟶

Have we said all there is to say? A voice rises to whisper in our ear that the soul poses a problem nevertheless, since there are some who simply deny its existence! Perhaps a definition of the soul proposed by Jacques de Bourbon Busset would be acceptable to almost everyone. Using a musical image, he says that the soul is the "continuo" of each being, the rhythmic music, almost in unison with the heartbeat, that each of us carries within from the time of our birth. It is located on a deeper, more intimate level than consciousness. Sometimes muted, sometimes hushed, it is never interrupted, and at certain moments of strong emotion or awakening, it makes itself heard. To make itself heard, to resonate, is its manner of *being*. To resonate, yes, that is the right word. To resonate within, to resonate with the "continuo" of another, to resonate with the "continuo" of the living universe, that is its chance to be immortal. "To sing is to be," asserts Rilke.[5] Does there exist any other law for the soul than this one: "Don't stop the music"?[6]

This preeminence assigned to the soul makes us think of courtly love as celebrated by the troubadours and, a bit later, by Dante and Petrarch. That almost mystical Western experience—though it existed in Arab and Chinese cultures—nevertheless seems suspect to some modern feminists. They see it as a "ruse," on the part of men who put women on a pedestal to better confine her, to fix her in an image, and thus to dominate her. I do not believe the trouvères and troubadours had such "Machiavellian" motives. Their adoration was not invented; it came from an authentic, irrepressible urge.

All the same, one point deserves to be emphasized. With such ardor, such respect, the adherents of courtly love make it clear that what they adore, more than the vulnerable, mortal woman, is that gift from afar that women in particular possess, a gift of beauty that is like divine grace.

Pronouncing these words, "gift" and "grace," I know that the moment has come to reflect upon the connection that can exist between beauty and goodness. Because I am of Chinese origin, I am also inhabited by my mother tongue. This heritage provides us with the expression *tian-sheng-li-zhi,* which means, "the beauty of the woman is a gift from heaven." Moreover, to designate the good, or goodness, the ideogram *hao* is composed graphically of the sign for woman and the sign for child. And most importantly, to designate beauty that is offered to our view, Chinese uses *hao-kan,* which means "good to see." Brought up with this language, the Chinese have an instinctive tendency to associate beauty and goodness. Thus why not note that in French as well, an intimate phonic tie exists between beauty (*beauté*) and goodness (*bonté*)? The two words come from the Latin *bellus* and *bonus,* which in fact derive from one shared Indo-European root: *dwenos.* Neither am I forgetting that in ancient Greek, a similar term, *kalosagathos,* contains both the idea of the beautiful (*kalos*) and the idea of the good (*agathos*). But most important, on the subject of the fundamental relationship between beauty and goodness, I would like to cite a passage from *La Pensée et le Mouvant,* by Henri Bergson. This passage is striking for its decisive simplicity: "It is grace that is seen through beauty and it is goodness that shows through grace. Because goodness is the infinite generosity of a principle (of life) that offers itself. These two meanings of the word grace merge into just one."[7]

If we want to return to Bergson's source, we can look again at Plotinus who, following Plato, distinguishes three stages in the ascent of the soul toward the Good: the soul begins by recognizing the beauty of perceptible things; then it ascends toward the world of mental forms and it seeks the origin of their beauty; finally it seeks to attain the Good, which is formless beauty, surpassing formal beauty.[8] We should make it clear that, according to Plotinus, beauty is linked to love. Love is a part of beauty and constitutes its supreme state, since beyond all the forms that beauty animates, what this love desires is the invisible light, the source of visible beauty. It is in this sense that we can understand Proust's statement:

"Beauty must not be loved for itself: because it is the fruit of the collaboration between the love of things and religious thinking."

I have just called upon some of the great thinkers. As for my own personal feelings, it seems evident to me that goodness is beautiful. Let us simply pose this question: Is there an act of goodness that is not beautiful? The answer is a given, so to speak, because in French one says *"un beau geste,"* and in Chinese one says "a beautiful virtue."

But is the reverse true? At first glance, that may seem less evident. Beauty, in the standard sense, is not necessarily good; we even speak of the "beauty of the devil." But let us not forget our basic criterion: true beauty is a matter of Being, which moves in the direction of open life. As for the beauty of the devil, based on deceit, playing the game of destruction and death, it is ugliness itself. We have insisted on this point from the beginning of our meditations. True beauty surpasses appearance, which again explains Plotinus's claim: "There is no beauty more real than the goodness one sees in someone. One loves him regardless of his face, which can be ugly [according to common sense]. One leaves his entire external appearance behind and seeks his [illuminating] internal beauty."[9]

Of course not all beauty attains perfect goodness, but all true beauty partakes of this essence, and tends toward supreme harmony, a notion that has the approval of all the sages since antiquity. By harmony, I do not mean simply what is appar-

ent in the arrangement of features that "objectively" constitute the presence of beauty. For me, harmony signifies above
all that the presence of beauty emanates harmony, radiating a
light of beneficence, which is the very definition of goodness.
It is no exaggeration to say that goodness and beauty form the
two faces of one organic, efficient entity. So what is the difference between them? Let us attempt a formula:

Goodness is the guarantee of the quality of beauty;
Beauty illuminates goodness and makes it desirable.

When the authenticity of beauty is guaranteed by goodness, it is in the supreme state of truth, which moves, let us
repeat, in the direction of open life, to which we aspire as
to something that is justified in and of itself. What is self-
justified in the order of life is, very much, beauty, which, rising toward the state of joy and freedom, allows goodness itself
to surpass the simple notion of duty. Beauty is the nobility of
the good, the pleasure of the good, the delight of the good,
the very radiance of the good.

We are forced to recognize, however, that, by some inexplicable aberration, the good is not valued in our times.
Misunderstood, it is reduced to something bothersome
because of its "good-natured" or "goody-goody" aspect.
Given our condition as "the damned on earth," occupied as
we are with suffering, fear, drab quotidian ugliness, and forever delinquent desires, with regard to beauty, we prefer to
exalt what is more perverse, what is more dramatic. Pessi-
mism, indeed even cynicism, thus assume the role of beauty;

they respond more effectively to our needs for derision and revolt.

Nevertheless, we must have the courage to return to goodness, to the true. Here I am thinking of the fierce, impetuous Beethoven. Speaking of his work and artistic creation in general, he was humble and lucid enough to say, "The true artist has no pride. . . . While others may admire him, he deplores having not yet arrived over there where a brighter genius shines for him like a distant sun. I recognize in no man no sign of superiority other than *goodness*. There where I find it, there is my home."[10]

The goodness that nourishes beauty cannot be identified with a few, more or less naive, good sentiments. It is exigency itself, the demand for justice, dignity, generosity, responsibility, elevation toward spiritual passion. Because human life is strewn with trials, eroded by difficulties, generosity requires ever-deeper engagement; as a result, it also deepens its own nature and engenders various virtues like sympathy, empathy, solidarity, compassion, commiseration, forgiveness. All these virtues imply a gift of self, and the gift of self is the gift that reminds us, once again, that the advent of the universe and life is an immense gift. This gift that keeps its promise and does not fail is, in itself, a moral code.

When this gift of self goes so far as to comprise the giving of one's life, with a view toward preserving intact the principle of life or saving the lives of others, that gift shines forth with a strange beauty. It signifies a supreme sense of justice, and the act so inspired conveys a courage full of nobility and grandeur. The most beautiful virtue in the eyes of the Confucians is to be "ready to die for what is but the *ren* [human love, the virtue of humanity]." This ideal is shared by all the great religions. One thinks of those who, to varying degrees, had to confront evil in the name of peace or love; one thinks—no matter what our conviction or belief—of Christ who, in order to show that absolute love is possible and that no evil can affect it, willingly accepted death on the cross. That was, without a doubt, one of the greatest "*beaux gestes*" that humanity has ever known.

On another level, we also think of all those innocent subjects of terrible moral or physical trials, especially if, through pain and suffering, they retain that share of light that rises from the human soul, and we are seized by that glimmer of beauty that shows through the emaciated, neglected face. Yes, beauty will never be able to make us forget our tragic condition. But there is a uniquely human beauty, that fire of the spirit that burns, if it burns, beyond the tragic.

All humans are not subjected to such trials. But all can partake of the grandeur arising from the inner dignity of those who confront the terrible, in the name of life. That is probably why, in Western art, the paintings representing the Pietà count among the greatest masterpieces. Let us consider the Avignon Pietà of the Louvre, one of the most impressive. This work, painted by Enguerrand Quarton in 1455, is the first great French example of panel painting. Caught up in no traditional school or technical precociousness, the artist put all the power of his soul into his work. The painting, which is very wide, has the dimensions of a triptych, but it is all one piece. The body of the crucified Christ is stretched horizontally across the length of the painting, a body stiffened and broken, the legs giving way, the right arm hanging, the fingers of the hand retracted. Around the body, three figures are positioned. On the right, John is bent forward over the head of Christ, while with his two hands, in a gesture of devotion that reflects a boundless filial love, he works to extract the thorns driven into the torture victim's skull. By Christ's feet, to the left, is Mary Magdalene. She is also bent forward, her left hand holding a flask of perfume. Her bloodred robe covers half the corpse (like blood flowing back). The bit of its lining with which she wipes her tears is yellow; it echoes the yellow rays that emanate from Christ's head. Though the woman's face is pale, we still see her cheek enflamed with passion and her lips parted as if she is still calling to the man, breathing words of love to him, never uttered, never interrupted.

In the center of the painting sits the Virgin. Her son's body is lying on her knees. She is dressed in a robe the color of dark night, which dramatically emphasizes the pallor of her face with its closed eyes and mouth. We can almost hear her silent cry of stunned grief. An upright bust, she is the only vertical figure in the painting, whereas the other two are positioned horizontally or obliquely. Rising in this way, she seems to be waiting, at the very core of her suffering, for a response from above.

Our gaze returns and refocuses on the emaciated body of Christ that forms the whole structure of the painting, that forms its backbone, so to speak, and almost, paradoxically, the line of force. We see that it is he who reunites and unites the living, pulling them into a movement of convergence and sharing. It is he who, having provoked tears of despair in all of them, alone seems capable now of drying those tears. This terribly stiffened, buttressed body suddenly becomes the expression of a noble intransigence, because it recalls the terrible resolution that its master adopted before death: resolving to prove that absolute love can exist and that no evil can alter or defile it.

Thus something begins to animate the whole painting: a held breath, of another order, is released through the wounds streaked with dried blood. A force asserts itself in our eyes: that body extended there is the result of a "*beau geste*," a gesture that has given rise to all the other gestures of John, Mary Magdalene, and Mary. The body had to be reduced to nearly nothing, laid bare by total deprivation, purified of all dross and heaviness, to be able to become the comforter again. It alone is capable of consoling now; that is its way of triumphing over death.

Beauty as redemption: Have we found the true meaning of Dostoyevsky's claim that "beauty will save the world"? To this claim, a contemporary, Romain Gary, responds: "I do not believe that there is a moral code worthy of man other than an aesthetic drawn from life, to the point of sacrificing life itself," and "It is necessary to ransom the world through beauty: the beauty of action, innocence, sacrifice, ideal."

FOURTH MEDITATION

UP UNTIL NOW, I have been conducting a personal meditation, relying for support from time to time on the words of one thinker or another. Later, we will approach the question of artistic creation and the possibility of establishing criteria for assessing value. For that I will have to call more systematically on the two great traditions of aesthetic thought, the Western and Chinese traditions, with which I am more or less familiar. For the moment, let us attempt to proceed in our investigation of the beautiful with the help of those theorists or practitioners from different cultural or spiritual traditions who have celebrated beauty. Inevitably, it is primarily from the West and China that I will draw themes and references, without neglecting a detour through Islam.

Let us begin, as we must, with Plato. In *The Symposium,* he shows how Eros, Love, follows a dialectical movement that ascends from the perceptible to the intelligible: from physical love, the object of which is the beauty of bodies, by way of moral love, the object of which is the beauty of the soul, all the way to the ultimate end: the contemplation of absolute beauty. Subsequently, over the course of Western history, those who grant beauty primacy use as their best authority the thinker who affirms that "beauty is the light of ideas," or, again, that "beauty is the splendor of the true."

Plato's heir, Plotinus, exalted beauty as a manifestation of the divine. Christianity had already made its debut. Also in this lineage fall Saint Augustine, Dante, and Petrarch. The feverish artistic creativity of the Renaissance, a veritable implosion of a desire long suppressed, was in itself a triumph of beauty. In the classical age, beauty certainly held a place of honor; it submitted to the demands of the true. "Nothing is beautiful but the true," Boileau was able to say.[1] The Romantics sought to reverse that order. They expressed their aspiration toward beauty, their conviction that the truth is linked to beauty, only to say that the supreme truth is nothing other than beauty.

Let us listen first to Alfred de Musset:

> *As for beauty, it is everything. Plato said so*
> *   himself:*
> *Beauty, on earth, is the highest thing.*
> *It is for us to reveal it as the light has.*
> *Nothing is beautiful but the truth, says a*
> *   famous verse;*
> *And I respond without fear of blasphemy:*
> *Nothing is true but the beautiful; nothing is*
> *   true without beauty.*[2]

As though to echo him, here are two famous lines of John Keats, the poet who said that "the earth is a valley where souls grow."[3]

> *Beauty is truth, truth beauty, —that is all*
> *Ye know on earth, and all ye need to know.*[4]

If we look to the Germans, we could cite Schiller or Novalis. But let us stay with Hölderin's injunction: "It is necessary to poetically inhabit the earth."[5] The poet invests great confidence in the power of poetic language. He is convinced that poetic language will allow us to accomplish the tasked assigned by beauty.

All these thoughts convey deep aspirations and convictions. They aim at forging a fundamental way of being. Nevertheless, without a sustained effort to define what true beauty is, they prove to be ineffective. However, we are not unaware of the theoretical advances of Fichte, or Schelling, their contemporaries, to whom we will turn in the next meditation. Still, it was not long after the Romantics and well before Nietzsche that the death of God was proclaimed, already, by Baudelaire, who inaugurated the modern era, as we say, and introduced into his work the anguish of the deracinated man lost in the Great City, haunted as he is by an awareness of ugliness and a fascination with evil.

⌒⌒

If we turn toward China, we can see that the founders of the two major currents of thought advanced the virtues of beauty from the beginning. Zhuangzi, one of the fathers of Taoism, in the fourth century BCE, pointed out that "between Heaven and Earth, there is great beauty" and that "nature has the power to transmute the withered and the rotten into marvels." The *zhen-ren*, the "true man" whom he proposes, is the one who, purified from within, is capable of entering into complete communion with the infinite realm of the universe, pursuing *shen-you* there, or "spiritual wandering."

Confucius is more concerned with man in society. His approach is primarily ethical. But to put into practice *ren,* "human virtue," he advocates *li,* "ritual," and *yue,* "music and poetry." *Li* promotes right relation, proper distance, as well as the beauty of bearing and gesture. *Yue* promotes the sense of measure and harmony. Moreover, Confucius dreams of making virtues as attractive as carnal desire. To do so, he appeals to the elements of nature that are both figures for beauty and symbols of certain virtues. He is known for expressions like:

"The intelligent man is fond of rivers, the compassionate man takes pleasure in the mountain," or again, "In the harshness of winter, one appreciates the vigor of the pines that stay green."[6]

Subsequently, in the texts and paintings of the literati, bamboo was celebrated for its elevated, upright nature, flowering cherries for blossoming in the snow, the orchid and lotus because they maintained the purity of their radiance even in the mud, and so on. Beyond these close ties between humanity and the world, where the good and the beautiful are united, we must also note the Confucianist triad: Heaven-Earth-Man. In this three-way relationship, it is as though the human represents an indispensable link. For the Confucianist human, if the human Way must proceed from Heaven and Earth, Heaven and Earth also need the Human to follow his Way in dignity.

It may be that the Confucians had too much faith in human nature; they reasoned very much in terms of good and evil, but they did not consider a fundamental question, that of extreme evil. In their conception of human relationships, they put great emphasis on duty, but they neglected to think about the problem of right, of the right that protects the individual as a subject with full freedom of consciousness. Nevertheless, this effort on the part of the best Confucians to respond to the appeal of the truth through the union of the good and the beautiful remains a position worthy of our attention.

Here, I would like to return to the three Platonic Ideas—the True, the Good, the Beautiful—with which we started. I think it is time to give up separating them into three categories and to reunite them, because the true, or truth, as it is currently used, in fact covers all of reality. Thus the truth no longer involves simply the great laws of life that allow it to function harmoniously according to the vital principle; it also applies to all forms of deviation and perversion, which take on extraordinary dimensions in our age and assail our consciousness. And the problem of extreme evil—evil capable of destroying the order of life itself—remains the inescapable hurdle in our attempts to establish values. So that this hurdle not be our single focus, so that it not block our view to the point of preventing access to a wider vision of a living universe that is a total gift, let us have the courage to give the highest place, in the scale of the true, to beauty based on goodness, as we defined it in the last meditation. In the highest place, the beauty in question represents the absolute value by which the other intermediate values can be established. I hardly use the word love, because the principle of love is contained within the principle of beauty, because love follows naturally from beauty, and because beauty moreover manifests what comes of love: communion, celebration, transfiguration.

Let us quickly add that this beauty, as an absolute value, is not in the least an unattainable star suspended in an ideal sky. It is within reach of humanity, but it is very much located, as we have said, beyond some state of delightfulness, of "good feelings." It includes taking charge of the suffering in the world, the rigorous demands of dignity, compassion, and a sense of justice, as well as the total opening to universal resonance. This exigency and openness require, on the part of the seeker, an effort to hollow out in oneself the capacity for receptivity and welcome, to the point of becoming the "ravine of the world," of letting oneself be burned by an intense light. This light alone is capable of making the rags encumbering body and mind fall away; it is the condition necessary for the advent of an authentic opening.

The process I have just described is, in reality, nothing other than the way of *Chan* (Zen) itself. This way affirms the value of our existence here and now, and thus the value of clear-sightedness. At the same time, it requires on the subject's part the constantly renewed resolve to divest, to the point of a state of nonseeing or nonbeing. It requires that the objective world be regarded directly, not according to its appearance, but as though at its roots, in such a way that the object truly takes root and grows in the very depths of the subject, and that, inversely, the me of the subject participates in the universal becoming. We can recall the Song master Qingdeng's three stages: see the mountain, no longer see the mountain, see the mountain again. Or again, the four stages of the Tang master Linji: face the object, no longer see the object, forget the self, object and self are born together.

This idea of being born together—which Claudel formulated in his own way—concurs with the experience of the Western thinker Henri Maldiney: "Sometimes awakening into the indecisive light of a corner of space, where all signs of recognition disappear, I perceive neither things nor images. I am not the subject of pure impressions, nor the indifferent observer of objects in front of me. I am co-nascent with [a] world that arises of itself and that dawns at my own dawning, which only arises with it."[7]

This way of awakening, which has inspired the most beautiful Chinese poems, is a basic mind-set for confronting the challenge of beauty as we understand it. And the elements that comprise this way are: gift, reception, bypassing appearance by dwelling in the full presence of the other, opening to the universal resonance.

Chan Buddhism makes me think, almost irresistibly, of another way, that of Orpheus, later enriched by Christianity. The first reason for this association may lie in the fact that, in Buddhism, there exists a similar legend, of Mu Lian, who goes to hell to save his mother. Despite a difference of degree, at their deepest levels, the two ways share the same spirit. Orpheus also understood that he had to "die himself" so that his way could attain the true dimension of the soul and resonate at the heart of the double realm of life and death (even in Paradise, Dante knows the state of remaining blind—canto 25—or of existing in the nonseeing—canto 30).

Let us repeat however that these two ways remain basic mind-sets. With regard to the profound nature of true beauty, it is necessary for us to advance further in our observations of its mode of existence and the complex relationship we maintain with it. Once again, we will look to China, drawing from that other experience what we need to nurture our meditation.

Throughout its history, Chinese culture has carried with it many variants and outdated elements that we can quickly put to one side. Its best part resides in a certain conception and a certain practice of life, and also in a certain experience of beauty. That part no Chinese is ready to abandon, whether he remains Confucianist or Taoist, whether he becomes Buddhist, Muslim, or even Marxist. It warrants our further consideration.

Chinese cosmology is based on the idea of the Breath, both substance and spirit. Beginning from this idea of the Breath, the first thinkers advanced a unitary, organic conception of the universe in which everything is linked and held together. The primordial Breath that ensures the original unity continues to animate all beings, linking them into a gigantic, interwoven, engendering network called the Tao, the Way.

Within the Way, the nature of the Breath and its rhythm are threefold in the sense that the primordial Breath is divided into three types of Breath that act concomitantly: the Yin Breath, the Yang Breath, and the Breath of the Median Void. Between the Yang, the active power, and the Yin, gentle receptivity, the Breath of the Median Void—which draws its power from the original Void—has the gift of pulling them into positive interaction, with a view toward a mutual transformation, as beneficial for one as for the other.

From this perspective, what passes between living entities is as important as the entities themselves. (That very ancient intuition reflects the thinking of the twentieth-century philosopher Martin Buber.) The Void here takes on a positive meaning, because it is tied to the Breath; the Void is the place where the Breath circulates and is regenerated. These three Breaths inhabit all living beings; however, each being is characterized by a more determinant pole of Yin or Yang. Let us cite, for example, the great entities that form pairs: Sun-Moon, Sky-Earth, Mountain-Water, Masculine-Feminine, and so on. Corresponding with this Taoist vision, Confucianist thought, as we saw earlier, is also threefold. The Heaven-Earth-Human triad affirms the spiritual role that humans must play within the cosmos.

This cosmological conception based on the Breath-Spirit has three consequences especially important to our way of apprehending the movement of life.

First consequence: because of the dynamic nature of the Tao, and especially the action of the Breath that ensures, from the beginning and in a continuous fashion, the processes that go from nonbeing toward being—or more precisely, in Chinese, from *wu* "there is not" toward *you* "there is"—the movement of life and our participation in that movement are always an ongoing, mutual outpouring, as at the beginning. In other words, the movement of life is perceived at each moment more as an advent or a "revival" than as a flat repetition of the same thing. To illustrate this kind of understanding, we can cite as examples two practices that have endured through time and are still vital: tai chi and calligraphy.

Second consequence: the movement of life takes place within a network of constant exchanges and interconnections. We can speak here of generalized interaction. Each life is connected, even without its knowledge, to other lives; and each life as a microcosm is connected to the macrocosm, the progress of which is none other than the Tao.

Third consequence: in the course of the Tao, which is anything but a repetition of the same, the effect of interaction is transformation. More precisely, in the interaction of Yin and Yang, the Median Void, drawing off the best part of them both, leads them into mutual transformation, as beneficial for one as for the other. Let us note that the Median Void acts in time as well. If the river is the image of time that flows without return, Chinese thought perceives that the water of the river, even while flowing, evaporates, rises into the sky to become a cloud, and falls down again as rain to renourish the river at its source. This cyclical movement produced by the Median Void is very much one of renewal.

Transposed to the level where our interest lies, the level of beauty's modes of existence, the three points above find their respective correspondences in the three following points:

- Beauty is always a becoming, an advent, if not to say an epiphany, and more concretely, an "appearance."
- Beauty implies interconnection, interaction, an encounter between the elements that constitute an occurrence of beauty, between the beauty present and the gaze that beholds it.
- From this encounter, if it is deep enough, something else arises, a revelation, a transfiguration, like a painting by Cézanne born of the encounter between the painter and the Sainte-Victoire mountain.

Not everyone is an artist, but each of us can be transformed, transfigured by the encounter with beauty, so true it is that beauty gives rise to beauty, increases beauty, heightens beauty. Beauty's function is threefold as well.

"Beauty is an appearance." This statement can be surprising. If beauty exists, is it not already there, whether one sees it or not? Why must it appear? The Chinese know that "objective" beauty exists. But they also know that living beauty is never static, never entirely revealed once and for all. As an entity animated by the Breath, it obeys the law of *yin-xian,* "hidden-revealed." In the image of a mountain hidden by the mist, or the face of a woman behind a fan, its charm resides in the unveiling. All beauty is singular; it also depends on circumstances, the moment, the light. Its revelation, if not its sudden arising, is always unexpected and unhoped-for. A beautiful face, even one we are used to, must present itself to us each time as new, as an advent. That is the reason why beauty always overwhelms us. It is a beauty full of gentle light that, suddenly arising above shadows and suffering, moves us to our very depths; other beauty, surging forth from underground, seizes or ravishes us with its strange spell; still other beauty, pure lightning, enthralls us, leaves us thunderstruck. . . .

I just evoked the image of the mountain hidden in mist. It makes me think of the expression "mist and cloud of Mount Lu," which means, in Chinese, true beauty—which is, as it must be, mysterious and unfathomable, as I have said. Celebrated for its mists and clouds, Mount Lu has moreover inspired two famous lines by the great fourth-century poet Tao Yuanming. Through its ingenious simplicity, this couplet explains the way the Chinese perceive beauty:

I gather chrysanthemums near the Eastern
    hedges
Here it is that, carefree, I perceive South
    Mountain.

The translated version only poorly conveys the first inter-
pretation of the couplet, which has a double meaning. In
effect, in the second line, the verb "perceive" is a translation
of *jian*. Now this verb in Ancient Chinese also means "to
appear," so that the second line can be read another way. In
place of "Here it is that, carefree, I perceive South Mountain,"
it can be read, "Here it is that, carefree, South Mountain
appears." We know that South Mountain—Mount Lu—only
reveals all the radiance of its beauty at the moment when the
mist suddenly disperses. Here, thanks to the double meaning
of the line, we are present at the scene of a marvelous encounter: toward evening, the poet bends down to pick chrysanthemums near the Eastern hedges; and suddenly, raising his head,
he perceives the mountain; but as the line suggests, his act of
perceiving the mountain coincides with the appearance of the
mountain itself, which, suddenly free of the mist, reveals itself
to his sight.

It happens, by happy coincidence, that in French as well
the word *vue*, view, has a double meaning: the view of the
one who is looking and the view of the thing being looked at.
Thus, in this particular case, the two views encounter each
other to form a perfect sufficiency, a miraculous state of sym-
biosis, all in a carefree way, as if through grace. The poet is
not that tourist who is anxiously watching for an opportune

moment to take a picture of the mountain. He knows that if he seeks to encounter the mountain in order to experience its beauty, he is also the long-awaited interlocutor.

We have just come one step closer to an idea of beauty that involves the intersection of a presence that offers itself to view and a view that captures it, an idea close to the concept of *chiasmus* proposed by Maurice Merleau-Ponty. The question of a moment ago arises once again: What, is there no objective beauty? Is it necessary for beauty to be seen for it to exist? My immediate response would be: objective beauty exists, but as long as it is not seen, it is fruitless. Nevertheless, not content with this response, let us try to head toward a more fundamental vision by making a detour through Chinese painting.

You have no doubt admired those Chinese landscapes in which, somewhere, a figure of minuscule dimension is perceptible. For the Western novice, whose eye is used to regarding works in which the subjects are represented in the foreground, thus relegating the landscape to the background, this figure is completely lost, drowned in the great whole. But that is not how the Chinese mind apprehends things. The figure in the landscape is always judiciously located: he is in the process of contemplating the landscape, playing the zither, or conversing with a friend. But after a moment, if we linger on him, we cannot fail to put ourselves in his place, and we realize that he is the pivot point around which the landscape is organized and turns, that it is through him we are seeing the landscape. Better yet, he is the awakened eye and the beating heart of the landscape. Once again, humans are not those external beings who build their sandcastle on a deserted beach. They are the most sensible, vital part of the living universe; it is to them that nature whispers its most constant desires, its deepest secrets. Thus a reversal in perspective is taking effect. At the same time as the human becomes the landscape's interior, so the landscape becomes the interior of man.

All Chinese painting, which is not a matter of naturalistic but of spiritualistic painting, is to be contemplated as the soul's landscape. It is as subject to subject, and from the perspective of intimate confidence, that man connects with nature there. This nature is no longer an inert, passive entity. If we regard it, it regards us as well; if we speak to it, it speaks to us as well. Evoking Jingting Mountain, the poet Li Bai affirms: "We regard one another tirelessly," which echoes the painter Shitao who, with regard to Mount Huang, says "Our tête-à-tête is endless." At all times in China, poets and painters are in this relationship of collaboration and mutual revelation with nature. The beauty of the world is an *appeal,* in the most concrete sense of the word, and humans, those beings of language, respond to it with all their soul. Everything occurs as if the universe, thinking to itself, were awaiting man to speak.

⟜⟝

Isn't all that only a dreamy illusion, an "oriental" whim? Does the Western individual, more rational, more skeptical, "master and possessor of nature," succumb to this "illusion"? The French expressions, "that speaks to me," "that sees me," or even "that says nothing to me," seem likewise to betray this need for an exchange of look and speech with the world. I am thinking here of the words of the painter André Marchand: "I have felt on certain days that it was the trees that were looking at me." How not to think of Cézanne as well? Some evenings he was moved to tears when he felt and saw, from Sainte-Victoire, that "geological ascent" from the original valley coming to meet the evening light in which each stone, each plant spoke to him in a native tongue. How not to think as well of Lacan who, as a child, on a pier one summer, was fascinated by a tin can floating on the water, sparkling in all its radiance. He had the clear awareness that it was the object that was drawing his attention to it and fixing him in its gaze.

Since I have spoken of the evening light with regard to Cézanne, let us advance further into observing the beauty of the sunset as we generally know it; this is an opportunity to verify the proposition according to which all true beauty we apprehend consists of intersection and interaction, that is to say, active encounters on many levels. Does the beauty in question consist of a simple ray of light emanating from the sunset? A simple light creates a luminous state that can be pleasant; but it in itself is still not beauty. When we say that the light is beautiful, it is because it sets the things it illuminates aglow, the sky more blue, the trees greener, flowers more glistening, walls more golden, faces more radiant. The light is only beautiful if it is incarnate. It is through stained-glass windows or rainbows that we can best admire the beauty of the light. The same is true for the sunset.

A sunset always takes place somewhere, on the sea, across

a plain, near a mountain. In this last case, we can imagine easily enough the basic elements of the landscape: the highest peak surrounded by smaller hills, the rocks intermixed with vegetation, the clouds that float close at hand or far off on the horizon, the birds that wheel in the rising mist, and so on. All of it, suffused with the last light of day, constitutes a moving scene. The beauty of the sunset is very much in the encounter of these elements. Nevertheless an encounter is more than an accumulation of things. Like a melody that, far from being an accumulation of notes, is formed by the consonance between the notes—"I look for the notes that love one another," said Mozart—the sunset transcends the elements of which it is organically composed, and each element finds itself transfigured there. And that is still only the encounter at the first level.

At a higher level, another encounter takes place when this scene is captured by the sight. If it is not captured by sight, such beauty does not know itself; it is "fruitless," it does not take on its full meaning. "To take on meaning" here means that the universe, each time it tends toward the state of beauty, offers an opportunity for—or renews a promise of—pleasure. The subject's gaze that momentarily captures the scene of beauty sparks a new encounter, located on another plane, the one of memory.

In the memory, or more precisely, in its duration, a subject's present gaze joins all his past encounters with beauty; it also meets the gaze of other creators whose works the subject has admired. This concurs with the truth I have already stated, that is, beauty attracts beauty, increases and heightens it. Beginning from there, from glance to glance, the subject may perhaps aspire—if inspired by the meeting—to a supreme encounter, one that would reunite him to the original gaze of the universe. Independent of any belief, he may feel instinctively that this universe, which was capable of engendering beings capable of vision, must possess vision itself. If the universe created itself, it had to "see itself" created, and eventually "speak itself": "that's beautiful," or more simply, "that's how it is." If this "that's beautiful" had not been spoken, would man have been capable of one day saying, "that's beautiful" themselves?

In light of these few reflections, we can understand that the gaze, exactly like the action of gazing, has nearly always gone hand in hand with time. This act, carried out by a subject, is, in effect, instantly accompanied by another effort, that of recognizing, which is linked to memory. In other words, what is gazed upon refers back, in the subject, to all that has been regarded by him in the past or in the imagination, and more deeply, to his intimate experience of a revelation of self spread out over time.

On this subject, I would like to recall a remark by Henri Maldiney, according to which the noun *regard* and the verb *regarder* are two words for which many languages can envy the French, because the combination of *re* and *garder* is rich with connotations. More than the fact of furtively capturing a view, an image, it evokes the retaking or the renewing of something that has been guarded and that demands, on each new occasion, to be disclosed as a becoming. Let us add, moreover, that *regard* includes the idea of *égard,* "consideration"; it always encourages the one who regards toward a deeper, more intimate engagement.

Does there exist a source for such *regard,* such looking, that would itself look? Even a culture as reputedly unreligious as the Chinese instinctively feels, as we have said, that this universe, which was capable of engendering living beings provided with eyes, must itself be moved by the need and the capacity to see. Also in Chinese, which means "to look, regard," includes the key to the sacred, the divine. Moreover, there is an almost clichéd expression deeply rooted in the imagination of the Chinese people: *lao-tian-you-yan,* "Heaven has its eyes." In this respect, we have just observed that the whole poetic and artistic tradition in China grew out of this fundamental conviction. Later, Buddhism introduced the notion of the "eye of wisdom," or the "third eye." The gaze engendered by this eye is more a matter of the universal consciousness that inhabits it than of the subject's wisdom, a consciousness that can only be acquired following the experience of emptiness.

We can solicit other testimony from other spiritual traditions, testimony from great mystics whose intuitions are, from our perspective, an authentic form of knowledge. If we turn our gaze toward the West, we can see that countless numbers have meditated on the theme of the human gaze— and by extension, the human face—in connection with the gaze of God. I will content myself with citing the words of Meister Eckehart, which later greatly interested Hegel: "The eye through which I see God is the eye through which God sees me."[8] From the great mystic's point of view, it follows that humans see the world that yields to vision as God sees it. The only difference is that God sees in it the hidden source and the invisible part. Humans can only gain access to this part through the soul. Let us recall that the word *Deus* comes from the word *dies,* which means "day" or "light of day." Thus, the light that renders visible the world always produces a dual perception for humans: the light makes seeing possible and the light itself is seen. Man longs to see them coincide with each other.

In many animals, the eyes are beautiful. In their innocence, human eyes are the most beautiful, according to Julien Green who notes in his *Journal:* "I wonder if in all the universe there exists anything that compares to them, what flower, what ocean? The masterpiece of Creation may lie therein, in the brilliance of their original color. The sea is no deeper. In this tiny abyss the most mysterious thing in the world shows through, a soul, and not one soul is exactly like another."[9]

With regard to Islam, there is a long tradition of meditating on the gaze and perception. Let us cite this passage from the Sufi master Sultan Valad, son of the great Rumi, in which the Creator addresses his creature, saying to him that it is through the soul, and not the body, that true perception is attained:

> Since your gaze is not pure enough to see my beauty unaccompanied and without an intermediary, I show it to you by means of forms and veils. Because your perception of what cannot be described comes by way of form; you can-

not see what is without alloy. Thus my beauty is alloyed
with form, in order to fall within your capacity for vision.
The universe resembles a body with its head in the sky and
its feet on the earth. Likewise, the human body has its sky
and stars; but this body lives through the soul. The eye,
the ear, the tongue live, see, hear, speak, feel thanks to the
soul. Vision, light, life, the faculties of perception: they all
come from the soul. It is through the intermediary of this
power of perception that we perceive the soul itself. When
the soul leaves the body, beauty, charm, and radiance no
longer remain in it. Know then that all beauty is made
manifest by the body, but it belongs to the soul.

Ibn Al-Arabi, one of the most renowned Sufi poets of
the thirteenth century, expressed the relationship between
the gaze of the Creator and that of his creature in his own
way. From quite a long poem, let us listen to the four following lines from which emerges a subtle dialectical vision. Here
again, it is the Creator speaking:

> *I created in you perception to be the object of my*
> *perception.*
> *It is through my regard that you see me and that*
> *I see you.*
> *You could not perceive me through yourself*
> *On the other hand if you perceive me, you*
> *perceive yourself, yourself.*

It seems obvious that the Creator created perception

in his creatures for them to be able to see him through his works. Nevertheless, the first line says that the Creator created perception in his creatures so that, most importantly, the creature can be the object of the Creator's own perception. Wouldn't the Creator have been able to create a creature without perception and have been content with watching this creature move, as one might amuse oneself with a toy? But that would not have been true perception. In the order of living beings, true perception takes place when a gaze encounters—or sees through—another gaze. Thus the Creator needs his creatures to be capable of seeing in order to be able to perceive them.

The second line elaborates further: it is through the regard of the Creator that the creature sees him. The creature encounters the Creator's regard and sees him. And at the same time, the Creator, encountering the gaze of the creature that sees him, sees the creature. The third line confirms this: the creature cannot see the Creator through itself. With the fourth line we understand that if the creature sees the Creator, it can truly see itself. We can also reverse what this line says, suggesting that, similarly, if the Creator sees the creature, he can truly see himself. In this long poem, if the Creator educates the creature about the mystery of the gaze, it is because he seeks to enter into a relationship of love with the creature. He asks the creature not to be content with regarding through itself alone; he literally implores the creature to meet his eyes. I use the verb *implore* on purpose, because I am thinking here of Phaedra who literally implores Hippolytus to look at her. We can recall Racine's lines in which we see how Phaedra, after having felt the beauty of Hippolytus's gaze, regrets that this gaze will not fall on her.

Perhaps more passionate, Rumi, that other mystic of Islam, instantly identifies any encounter with the divine gaze as an act of love. This exchange of love offers to totally confuse the regarding with the regarded, that is to say, the lover and the beloved:

> *The one whose beauty is such that all are jealous*
> *of him*
> *Came this night, weeping for my heart*
> *He wept and I wept, until the dawn came*
> *He said: It's strange, of the two of us, who is the*
> *lover?*

In love as in beauty, any true gaze is a mutual gaze. That is why Merleau-Ponty defines perception through the concept of *chiasmus,* precisely that interpenetration between what regards and what is regarded. An isolated gaze only achieves beauty with difficulty. Mutual gazes alone can produce the spark that illuminates, and in the extreme case of the Creator and his creature, alone can allow the divine light to be revealed. But in an authentic experience of love and beauty, isn't any creature elevated to the rank of the Creator, since it is true that exchanged looks give rise to them both, make them both *be*? Perhaps that is the deep meaning of the quatrain by Angelus Silesius (*The Cherubic Wanderer*):

My God, if I did not exist
You would no longer exist
Since me you are not
With this need that you have for me[10]

At a superior level, the gaze goes beyond a fascination with the face and attains the light of the soul that is true presence. This light received from without penetrates within and becomes interior light that makes visible the soul of the other and the soul of the self in a vision made of give and take, like a fountain of crossed jets. At that moment, the eyes are closed as in prayer, or in ecstasy.

Here I am thinking of those Khmer heads that can be viewed at the Guimet Museum. We no longer see their eyes, but curiously we see their gaze turned toward the infinite space of the interior. On the subject of this infinite interior space, let us add one point. If one confines oneself to the physical body, this is a terribly restricted space. If one admits to and accepts the spiritual body, that is to say, the body animated by the Breath of the spirit, there is virtually infinite space, even though this spiritual body still needs to be awakened and to enter into an exchange, in resonance with the Breath that animates the living universe. That is because the infinite is what ceaselessly bursts forth toward open life. But the interior space cannot be ignored. It is a necessary means, and it is from there that everything can once again radiate.

The dimension in question is truly the one of the soul. It is deep within interior space that one can hear the voice of the soul, that one can perceive the vision of the soul. Observing a Khmer head in contemplation, we can see that we have before us a face entirely absorbed by the regard, a face that becomes pure gaze and pure smile, a face of vision where visible and invisible nurture one another, where the source of beauty and actual beauty are one and the same. Turned inward, then turned outward again, this face may thus radiate another light, the light of transfiguration.

FIFTH MEDITATION

UNTIL THE BEGINNING OF the twentieth century, artistic creation came under the sign of the beautiful. The models for beauty could be adapted according to the eras; the aim of art remained the same: to celebrate and reveal beauty, to create the beautiful. As early as the end of the nineteenth century, and throughout the twentieth, many factors converged to change this order: the ugliness of big cities resulting from frantic industrialization, the awareness of "modernity" based on the idea of "the death of God," the collapse of humanism prompted by successive tragedies on the global scale. All these elements turned the traditional conception of art on its ear, so that it was no longer limited to the exaltation of beauty recognized as such. Through a sort of generalized expressionism, artistic creation, following the example of literature, which had experienced an earlier awakening, meant to come to terms with the entire reality of living beings and the entire human imagination. No longer aimed exclusively at beauty, except on the level of style, it willingly resorted to the most extreme ruptures and distortions.

Nevertheless, despite the general impression of an unleashing of "sound and fury," the golden thread of the beautiful was not entirely broken. To cite only the most well-known painters, both "figurative" and "abstract": Braque, Matisse, Picasso, Chagall, Miró, Bonnard, Derain, Marquet, Morandi, Balthus, de Staël, Kandinsky, Delaunay, Bazaine, Hartung, Sam Francis, Rothko, Manessier, Soulanges, Zao Wou-Ki. Through them, or above them, reference to the past remains viable.

I would like to note here the perspective of a man who has an acute sense of the modern tragic, the poet-painter Max Jacob. In his *L'Homme de cristal,* he writes in all simplicity:

> *On my death mask my studies will be read*
> *and all that enters of all the nature*
> *in my heart aspiring to all beauty,*
> *travels, peace, the sea, the forest.*[1]

And in *Derniers poèmes,* he evokes his nostalgia: "It is enough that a child of five, in his pale blue smock, drew in a sketch book so that some door opened in the light, so that the castle was rebuilt and the ochre of the hill was covered with flowers."[2]

An artistic creation worthy of its name, taking a hard look at the whole of reality, must maintain both intentions. It must of course express the suffering, violent part of life, as well as all the forms of deviation that this life engenders, but it also has the task of continuing to reveal what the living universe harbors of virtual beauty. In short, each artist must achieve the mission Dante assigned: to explore both hell and paradise. Moreover, one of the proofs of this virtual beauty's existence is found in artistic creation itself. In artistic creation, the search for the beauty of form and style—even if this beauty is, necessarily, never sufficient—is the mark that distinguishes a work of art from other human productions with more utilitarian purposes. Authentic art is in itself a conquest of the spirit; it elevates man to the rank of the Creator, it makes leap from the shadows of destiny a flash of emotion and memorable pleasure, a gleam of passion and compassion that can be shared. Through its constantly renewed forms, it tends toward open life by breaking down the barriers of habit and prompting a new way of perceiving and living.

When I speak of art, I have in mind music as much as poetry and painting. I grant Western music a place of eminence, to say the least. In all these domains, human genius has been able to attain its highest degree of expression. That is because art is always the crystallization of an apparently provisional "here and now," the elevation of a presence in time as advent. These achieved forms that reactivate the great rhythms are the highest means by which humans can defy destiny and death. That does not in any way undercut the value of other types of activities and work. Quite simply, art possesses the gift of justifying itself through its own existence, through "the thing itself." Man can draw from it a raison d'être for their earthly existence. How not to think of Baudelaire's famous lines:

> It is a cry repeated by a thousand sentinels,
> An order passed on by a thousand messengers;
> It is a beacon lit on a thousand citadels,
> A hunters' cry lost in the great woods!

⌒◦⌒

> Because truly, Lord, it is the best evidence
> That we can offer of our dignity
> This ardent sob that rises from age to age
> And comes to die on the shore of your eternity![3]

Here the poet pays homage to the great painters that produced the glory of Western pictorial art. I will take a very similar approach. Without neglecting worthy examples from the various artistic domains, I do tend to emphasize painting because, with regard to the beautiful, this visual art form impresses us with its powerful evidence. It really is painting that has given rise over the course of the centuries to the most concrete reflections, and the most consequential as well. That is why, in my own reflections, I will call upon the two traditions of thought that I know something about, the Western and Chinese traditions, as I began to do in the last meditation. This time, I will examine aesthetic thought—or the philosophy of art. In particular, my goal is to determine the extent to which it is still possible to extricate a few notions of value for defining the beautiful as engendered by artistic creation, despite the total confusion in which we have found ourselves for a century now.

Let us point out that this is not in the least a matter of a systematic study; the present framework does not permit that. Concentrating on overlooking no detail and hiding behind cumbersome scholarly apparatus can only serve as means for evading what seems to me essential. My goal is not to oppose the East and the West, one more time and in some rigid fashion, emphasizing their differences in order to flatter some narcissistic tendency on one side or the other. That has already been done. If we get no further than that, the game proves to be futile. I will endeavor, of course, to bring out those differences, but by viewing them as complementary. Can we deny that, because of the uniqueness of beings and cultures, diversity is the very condition of being human, in all its richness and good fortune?

Nevertheless, I have lived long enough to observe and understand that, at its very depths, the human effort to reach toward the beautiful is universal in nature. Thus I have no doubt that the definitive dialogue marking the coming century will take place not in the spirit of confrontation, but of understanding, the only way that matters. Regarding Western aesthetic thought, with which everyone is familiar, I will only mention a few points that seem important to me. If I pay greater attention to Chinese aesthetic thought here, that does not reflect a preference. Quite simply, with a view toward a more comprehensive dialogue, I am interested in contributing the piece with which I am most familiar.

⌒ ◦ ⌒

With regard to the major current of thought dominant in the West, from the Greeks up to the rationalism of the modern age, and by way of Descartes, one could say very schematically that what distinguished it, and what, in many respects, made it great—even if, for a century now, its limits on the philosophical plane have been under scrutiny—is its dualistic approach: a dualism based on the separation between spirit and matter, subject and object. This separation was a necessary stage, which had some positive outcomes beneficial to all humanity. The affirmation of the object to be observed and analyzed resulted in logic and scientific thinking. As for the affirmation of the subject, it resulted in the development of rights that protect the subject's status, in real freedom.

Though it has given rise to some very fertile thinking in the area of aesthetics, this overly rigid separation has not always encouraged a kind of approach that envisions an organic process in which subject and object are involved in a continuous give and take, continually producing reciprocal transformation. Throughout the course of thought that seeks to define the phenomenon of artistic creation and to establish criteria for beauty, it is as though there is an oscillation, or an indecisiveness, between the preeminence of the object and that of the subject. To greatly oversimplify, we could say that, from Greek antiquity to the eighteenth century, the ideal for beauty governing artistic creation endeavored to find its basis in objective criteria, art modeling itself on the most enlivening, inspiring, and noble aspects of Nature.

In his *Phaedrus,* Plato says that beauty is manifested in things through their "integrity, simplicity, immobility, felicity, which belong in their turn to appearances that, through initiation, are unveiled to us in a pure and radiant light."[4] In his *Metaphysics,* Aristotle adopts the same position, even while formulating more concrete criteria: "The highest forms of the beautiful are order, symmetry, definition, and it is there especially that the mathematical sciences make their appearance."[5] These objective principles of order, symmetry, and definition, which lead to the idea of much sought-after harmony, desired contrast, just proportion, remain uncontested rules. Later, the baroque styles certainly constituted a form of liberation, though without calling into question the basic rules.

In various eighteenth-century Western European countries, people began to rethink the issue of beauty in art. In his article on the beautiful, Diderot, an admirer of Chardin, still takes a fundamentally classical approach, with a few breakthroughs in the direction of a new perspective, when, touching on the inner structure of a work, he maintains, as we saw earlier, that the beauty emanating from it resides in *relationships,* or when he proposes the idea that, beyond *imitation,* art teaches us to see in Nature what we do not see in reality.

It is in the article on genius that he proves the most bold: "The Genius is an autonomous, free subject, creator of his own laws. Any rule or constraint erodes his creative power to produce pathos, the wild, and the sublime."

Nevertheless, for the eighteenth century, it is really to Germany that we must turn once again. That is where an exceptional moment in philosophy occurred, known as German Idealism. From the mid-eighteenth until the first decades of the nineteenth century, three generations of thinkers succeeded one another to undertake an inquiry into the subject that concerns us here—a passionate, fascinating quest that would spark the literary and artistic movement known as Romanticism. It would serve the rest of our meditation well to summarize this experience, be it in a perfunctory and inevitably clumsy way.

Let us begin, as we must, with Baumgarten, born in 1714, a disciple of Wolff's and exact contemporary of Winckelmann's, author of the famous *History of Art and Antiquity*. He is credited with being the first to express the wish that a discipline be established related to aestheticism, a kind of science of sensibility, beauty being in his eyes the sensible form of truth. Immediately following him, the German thinkers would make it their duty to reflect upon the question of beauty.

Kant himself is no exception. To his great "critiques," he would add a *Critique of Judgment,* devoted to the way man apprehends beauty. In this admirable work of precision and clarity, the philosopher's point of view is that of a spectator who finds himself before an object of beauty or a work of art, and who is trying to appreciate it. This is not quite the perspective of a creator engaged in the process of creation whose consciousness confronts beauty as a challenge directed at it. That is only logical, because the philosopher's general approach is "dualistic." He is in the position of a subject who approaches the object before him with the intention of knowing it. We know how lucidly he was able to assess the limits of human knowledge. Nevertheless, we also know that his philosophical reflections led him to wonder whether "the thing itself," the thing as it exists in and of itself, can be known by man.

For the philosopher, our taste is the basic element that allows us to judge beauty, and Kant goes on to give us four definitions of the beautiful: "The beautiful is the object of disinterested satisfaction"; "The beautiful is that which universally pleases without concept"—that is, beauty cannot be proved, only experienced; "The beautiful is the final form of an object as it perceived without final representation"—that is, a work of art does not aim toward a useful end; "The beautiful is that which is recognized without concept as the object of a necessary satisfaction"—that is, each of us must necessarily be sensitive to it.[6]

From our perspective, these four definitions are probably not sufficient to apprehend how entirely shattering beauty is, the entire potential transformation that takes place within when a subject's spirit and desire are grappling with beauty.

In reaction to his teacher Kant, Fichte maintains that to a certain degree we can know the "thing itself," to the extent that this is basically the same as the mind knowing the man. Exalting the reflective subject who draws from within himself the resources of knowledge, he builds a system that finally becomes an absolute idealism in which there is no reality other than the I.

Reacting in his turn to his teacher Fichte, Schelling in some way completes the intense dialectical play that takes place over three generations. Schelling is fully conscious of the importance of the knowing, acting, creating subject. He also knows that a subjectivism without "safeguards" lapses into the arbitrary and leads in a direction contrary to the truth of life. Human consciousness must not be a chimerical accomplice or a bloodless opponent, but a partner, an interlocutor. This role cannot be arbitrarily chosen, dependent on our goodwill. It must be the very source of life. And for Schelling, Nature is given a meaning much like the one the Greeks gave to the word *physis*. According to him, Nature, in its potential, unrevealed depths, is not just a passive, servile entity, a simple source of basic materials, or worse, a decorative backdrop for mankind. It is the primitive cosmic force, a matter of a sacred, eternally creative principle. In entering into a continuous, exacting dialogue with it, man is assured of his place in the authentic way of life and Creation.

The essence of Schelling's thinking can be found in his work *System of Transcendental Idealism,* published in 1800. He gives true artistic creation the highest place, even above pure philosophical speculation. He endeavors to show that, eager to know the absolute, the spirit that inhabits man is engaged in a quest for the identity of the self and of the world. This higher identity in which the self and the world coincide can only be realized through art. That is because, in the act of creation, the artist objectifies the idea in the material, and thus subjectifies the material as well. Thus art unites opposites as apparently irreconcilable as spirit and nature, subject and world, individual and universal. The work that achieves greatness contains infinite intentions and possibilities; it is truly the face of the infinite in the finite, the only place where the contradictions are resolved through appeasement.

Among all the Western thinkers, Schelling's vision of art comes closest, in my view, to the one underlying Chinese arts and letters, even if, for Chinese thought, the notion of "absolute identity" embraces something too fixed, too static. Unfortunately, Schelling's thinking was soon overshadowed by that of his fellow student Hegel, whose genius would sweep aside all in its path.

The fragile equilibrium based on man's respect for the Other—Nature or the living universe—and on the sincere and beneficial exchange between two interlocutors would be upset by Hegel's overwhelming system. We know, of course, all the greatness of Hegel's thought; nevertheless, we dare to propose this: by anticipating the triumph of the absolute Idea, which, according to the philosopher, will lead to the disappearance of artistic creation and religion, the object, as a negation that allows the subject-spirit to surpass itself, seems nothing more than a kind of "provisional springboard," a "utilitarian pretext." It is not, as with Schelling, an entity that, offering contradictions and constructive demands, would be destined to endure. If we admit that, especially in art, the essential thing is what arises between the interlocutors according to the principle of life, in view of a shared transformation, then the

Hegelian dialectic is not, strictly speaking, "dialogue"; it does not follow a true threefold movement.

After Hegel, in the area of aesthetic thought, Nietzsche exalted the vital energy of Dionysian inspiration, while Benedetto Croce advocated the subjective expression of the human spirit. Paradoxically—or fortunately—during this same period, the artists themselves, and especially the impressionists, instinctively understood the need to resume authentic dialogue with Nature. Pissarro, Monet, Van Gogh, Gauguin, Renoir, Sisley—each, in his way, followed his vision to its end, invigorated by the inexhaustible resources of Nature, rediscovered.

Without meaning in the least to compare him to the others, I will nevertheless concentrate on the case of Cézanne, who, it seems to me, achieved great depths when he undertook painting the rocks and trees of Sainte-Victoire. Beyond atmospheric time, he plunged into a geologic time, and witnessed, from within, that ascent of telluric power from its original darkness to the light of day, to the rhythmic unfolding of what the earth bears within itself as varied forms, rendered more varied still by that fascinating play of light radiating from the sun.

For Cézanne, beauty results from encounters on all levels. On the level of represented Nature, it is the encounter between the hidden and the revealed, between the moving and the fixed; on the level of the artistic act, it is the encounter between brushstrokes, between the colors applied. And beyond all this, there is the decisive encounter of the human spirit and the landscape at a privileged moment, with something trembling, vibrating, unfinished in that interval, as if the artist has made himself the repository or host, awaiting the coming of some visitor who knows how to inhabit what is captured, offered.

Yes, as the twentieth century dawns in the West, this singular figure arises, with whom the great Song and Yuan masters across the centuries would willingly converse. Undeniably, Cézanne's work is closest to the great landscape tradition in China. It offers enough breadth to serve as meeting place where the two traditions can recognize and enrich each other, and do so from the perspective of mutual renewal. With regard to Western art, cubism only exploited a superficial part of all the richness contained in this work.

It is no surprise that, following the advent of phenomenology—that attempt to "return to things"—Merleau-Ponty wanted to study the phenomenon of perception and creation according to the experience of Cézanne. Spending a summer at the base of the painter's Mount Sainte-Victoire, he observed that the act of perception and creation arose from chiasmus—a notion that we have already mentioned several times—a chiasmus created by the intersection of gazes, which leads to the intersection of bodies and minds. In this play of complete encounter, the gazing subject is no less gazed upon, since it is true that the regarded world also reveals itself to be a "regarder." The intersection between the two entities facing each other is transmuted into interpenetration. It is very much body to body and mind to mind that true perception-creation takes place.

Again within the intellectual realm of phenomenology,

even though he never acknowledged this kinship, Heidegger also drew certain lessons from Cézanne and, less directly, from Lao-tzu. Meditating upon the nature and significance of a work of art, he appealed to the image of the empty vase, among others. This image, in its very simplicity, nevertheless connects to Earth and Heaven, the human and the divine. Any work of art worthy of its name is endowed with that "connective" power. We cannot help but hear an echo of Schelling's philosophy here, which Heidegger studied in depth.

All this relates to the general direction of Western thinking on artistic creation. This thinking, of course, pursued further concrete investigations of artistic practice. Relying on a solid history of art, it proposed some elements for distinguishing styles and genres, some models for defining forms and structures, some rhetorical figures—metaphor, metonymy, allegory, symbol, and so on—to describe the multiple processes involved in producing a work. I would like to go back now, just briefly, to two primary ideas that determined the orientation of Western art, that is, mimesis and catharsis.

⌒◦⌒

The term *mimesis* (imitation) has given rise to numerous interpretations. I will limit myself here to the meaning that Plato and Aristotle give it. In Plato's philosophy, *mimesis* has two slightly contradictory meanings: on the one hand, it is the art of "true" reproduction; on the other hand, it is an art of illusory appearance. If the artist reproduces a work conforming to the values of proportions for the human body, he or she creates a true work. In this regard, let us point out that the major artistic form in ancient Greece was sculpture, which above all celebrates the human body. In that idealized figure of beauty and desire, behind which one feels the divine hand, appearance and substance converge.

On the other hand, when the artist distances herself from the objective truth, she creates a work in which resemblance is only artifice, illusion, and pretense. This art of deception is condemned by Plato; that is why painters and poets will be excluded from the ideal city, as the philosopher conceives of it in *The Republic*.

Aristotle rejects the dichotomy established by Plato, and maintains in his *Poetics* that the principle of all the arts lies in mimesis. The philosopher knows that art proceeds by way of form through matter, that the artist who works with matter to give it form will inevitably be led to master matter and form, and to know them. This permits him to assert that the work of mimesis is a process of knowledge.

Thus the artist adopts this initial stance inspired by the emphasis on reproduction that determined the spirit of Western art. The artist capable of reproduction delights in his technical feats; the artist capable of knowing matter and re-creating form continually feeds his desire for mastery over the world. The idea of mimesis exists in all cultures, but it is in the West that its practice has had extreme consequences, thanks undoubtedly to that very early dawning of its particular significance. If we look at Western painting and sculpture overall—leaving aside music—up until the nineteenth century, it seems possible to extricate the line of force: rather than creating a dream state or one of pure communion, the dominant tendency aims at mastering reality through accurate representation.

The spirit that animates this art is one of conquest. I do not use this term in a pejorative sense at all. It is true that an exclusive, exaggerated spirit of conquest blinds the creator and prevents him from accomplishing the whole task that art assigns him. Nonetheless, the better part of this spirit has made Western art great. It is the greatness of knowledge. Practical knowledge first of all: minute observations of optical effects and atmospheric phenomena; analysis of the composition of mineral, vegetable, and animal matter. And conquest of conquests: the precise formulation of the laws of perspective.

But it is knowledge of another order that we want to emphasize here. Heir to the Greek and Judeo-Christian tradition, Western art has tirelessly represented landscapes where the dramas and aspirations of mankind, the very body of man, are played out, the carnal body in all the radiance of pleasure, of course, but also the violent, suffering body, victim of cruelty and derision, the body offered up for sacrifice and the hope of redemption.

Beyond landscapes and bodies, Western art, among all the arts in the world, has looked hardest at the face, most scrutinized all the facets of its mystery: the moving mystery of its beauty, the no-less-incredible mystery of its ability to slip into hideous grimaces. Between beauty and hideousness a whole gamut of expressions are concentrated in the face, through which a life unrevealed seeks to be expressed: tenderness, rapture, jubilation, desire and pursuit, ecstasy, solitude, melancholy, anger, desolation, despair. . . . Among all those who have probed this mystery, Rembrandt, who comes after the great Renaissance painters, certainly deserves the place of eminence.

As to the idea of catharsis, it was also explored by Aristotle, in connection with the passions in his *Poetics*. It is to the theater, and to tragedy in particular, that this Greek term is linked, *catharsis* meaning "purgation," in the almost medical sense of the term "purge," and in a more elevated sense of "purification." The spectator, witnessing the performance of a tragedy, participates in it mentally. He can experience all kinds of feelings, of which the dominant ones will be fear and pity. He experiences relief when at the end of the drama the injustice is redressed, or the criminal is tortured by remorse, or punished. If the tragedy succeeds in plumbing the mystery of human destiny, and if the spectator experiences "sacred fright," the purification that results can be understood as an inner reversal, a spiritual elevation.

Whatever evolution occurred in the development of classical Greek tragedy—an evolution that sees fate's predominance superceded by the struggle of the human conscience—the sacred is present there. It is especially the voice of the chorus that comments on the action, lamenting or praising it, and that invokes the divine powers, which offer a distant and intransigent face, from which arises the dramatic tension. This is the means for measuring the human by the yardstick of the divine; the mortal condition is apprehended by the light of the gods. Here, death appears as the ultimate end point, and at the same time, paradoxically, as the very hope of a beyond. In effect, it is offered as the single chance for redemption or transfiguration. Underlying all the tragedies, the myth of Orpheus remains, prefiguring the passion of Christ that will haunt the Western imagination, beyond all questions of belief.

In this light we see that certain human tragedies can only be transmuted into beauty through a spiritual reversal and a transfiguration. From my perspective, Greek tragedy lays the foundation. It contributes to the greatness of which we have spoken; later it will permeate all forms of the artistic tradition: theater, literature, painting, music, dance.

Given Western art's ceaseless development and the long theoretical tradition that accompanied it, I hardly see how Chinese art can be compared to it. For nearly three millennia, China has experienced artistic creation with remarkable continuity. No less remarkable is the fact that it has accumulated, over the course of these long centuries, an impressive body of theoretical texts coming from thinkers and then from artists themselves. That is especially true in the areas of poetry, calligraphy, and painting. These three arts have maintained an organic relationship. They would form a unified practice when so-called literati painting developed in the eleventh century. Henceforth the literati painters would adopt the habit of including in their paintings calligraphed poems. This art trio took the expression of the human spirit to such heights that the Chinese finally came to consider them the supreme form of human accomplishment.

Observing this particular tradition, I would be tempted to paraphrase Kant, but in the reverse. I would say that the knowledge of the beautiful is universal and founded on concepts; that it is disinterested but has a purpose. Because, curiously, it is in poetic theory, and even more so in pictorial theory, both of them nurtured by practical experience, that Chinese thinking engendered the greatest number of ideas, some of which, of general import, are true concepts.

As to the purpose of beauty, at least the beauty that art produces—art that, in fact, draws its essence from the beauty contained in Nature—the Chinese of the classical age were convinced that the truest life earthly destiny offers is found there. The purpose of artistic beauty in its highest state is more than "aesthetic" pleasure; its function is to give life. Didn't the great eleventh-century painter Guo Xi say that "many paintings exist to be looked at, but the best are those that offer mediumistic space so that one can sojourn there indefinitely"? In this sojourn of another order, to die means to return to the invisible.

Such long-lived conviction, despite significant gaps, and such lived experience, may deserve a moment's attention. It is a piece to add to record of the great dialogue that finally began between the Far East and the West. Within the limited framework of the present meditation, I will mention only three fundamental notions: *yin-yun,* "unifying interaction," *qi-yun,* "rhythmic breath," and *shen-yun,* "divine resonance." The three of them, linked to one another in an organic, hierarchical way, constitute three levels, or three degrees, of a criterion beginning from which the Chinese tradition proposes to judge the value of a work, and thus, the truth of beauty in general.

But before addressing them, we must make a detour, recalling—even if it means repeating—what we have said so far on the subject of Chinese thought and the particular spirit of its approach. Repetition serves some useful purpose here in that it allows us to confirm some important points even while advancing a few steps further. Thus let us repeat the following ones. Beginning with the idea of *qi,* "Breath," simultaneously matter and spirit, the first Chinese thinkers proposed a unitary, organic conception of the living universe in which everything is linked and interdependent. The Breath constitutes the fundamental unity, and at the same time it continually animates all the beings in the living universe, connecting them into a giant network of life-in-process called the Tao, the Way. Within the Tao, the operation of the Breath is threefold, in the sense that the primordial Breath is divided into three types, the interaction of which governs the whole of living beings, that is, the Yin Breath, the Yang Breath, and the Breath of the Median Void. The Yang Breath, embodying active power, and the Yin Breath, embodying receptive gentleness, need the Breath of the Median Void—which, as its name indicates, embodies the necessary intermediary space of encounter and circulation—to enter into effective, and insofar as is possible, harmonious interaction.

This brief survey reminds us, if such a reminder is necessary, that from the beginning, the dominant current in Chinese thought—the "Median Void" for the Taoists, the "Golden Mean" for the Confucians—sought to overcome dualism. Today we see more clearly what Chinese thought has lacked and what China must learn from the West. On the other hand, from the perspective of aesthetic theory—regarding the beautiful, and in particular artistic creation—China seems to have been very precocious. This threefold thinking comprehended very early that beauty is precisely of a threefold nature. As we have said, the Chinese were quite aware that "objective beauty" existed, and they had no lack of words to characterize it. But in their eyes, true beauty—beauty that occurs and is revealed, that just suddenly appears to touch the soul of the one who perceives it—results from the encounter between two beings or between the human spirit and the living universe. And the work of beauty, always arising from a "between," is a third thing that, springing from the interaction of the two, allows the two to surpass themselves. If there is transcendence, it lies in this surpassing.

Still on the subject of the threefold spirit, it is worth noting that in the Chinese rhetorical tradition, and subsequently in aesthetics, ideas or illustrations often come in pairs. Coupled, like "Yin-Yang," "Heaven-Earth," "Mountain-Water," for example, the binomial is the very expression of the threefold, since it expresses the idea that each of the figures conveys, but also the idea of what takes place between them, offering them the possibility for surpassing themselves. Thus, occupying a dominant place is the rhetorical pairing *bi-xing,* "comparison-incentive," and later, the pair *qing-jing,* "feeling-landscape."

The first pair, *bi-xing,* "comparison-incentive," forms part of the tradition of commentaries on the *Book of Songs*. This work is the earliest collection of poetry in Chinese literature. Compiled in the sixth century BCE—probably by Confucius—it contains pieces that go back more than a millennium before our era. The opus of over three hundred poems gave rise, a few centuries later, to a tradition of commentaries. The function of the two principal figures that form this first pair was to analyze the poetic processes. More than simple rhetorical figures, in reality, they were true philosophical notions, to the extent that they advanced the relationship of subject and object. The *bi,* "comparison," designates the case in which the poet chooses from Nature an element to illustrate or embody his sensations or feelings, thus, a movement going from the subject toward the object; the *xing,* "incentive," designates the case in which a natural scene produces in the poet's innermost depths a memory, an emotion, thus, a movement going from object to subject. Combined, they form a pair that gives rise to a process of give and take governing the coming of poetry, which cannot be purely subjective projection or purely objective description. From the Chinese perspective, poetry, that meaningful practice, is a matter of putting into relationship, at great depths, the human being and the living universe, which is considered to be a partner, a subject.

The second pair, *qing-jing,* "feeling-landscape," came into its own later. It comes, so to speak, to enlarge the field of application of the first pair, while providing it with a more dynamic content. In effect, this second pair applies as much to poetry as to painting and music. It further emphasizes the dialectical relationship of reciprocal becoming between man and Nature: the human feeling can unfold in the landscape, and for its part, the landscape is endowed with feeling. The two of them are engaged in a process of mutual transformation and shared transfiguration.

Beginning from these two pairs that are the basis for Chinese poetics, theoreticians over the centuries have not neglected the detailed analytic work of distinguishing genres and styles as well as the various sorts of inspiration, modes of expression, and so on.

But, let us not stray too far from our main subject.

After this long detour to review the foundations of Chinese thought and a few points on Chinese poetics, the moment has finally come to address the three fundamental ideas that we mentioned at the beginning, that is, *yin-yun,* "unifying interaction," *qi-yun,* "rhythmic breath," and *shen-yun,* "divine resonance." According to the Chinese aesthetic, any work of art worthy of the name—more precisely, painting and poetry—must possess the qualities designated by these ideas. They can thus serve as criteria for judging the value of a work.

Here, we are momentarily seized by doubt again. Can criteria really be proposed for judging the value of a work of art? Isn't the generally accepted notion of "individual taste" enough to discourage any effort in this direction? Moreover, every work of art has a form. Form can prevail over content and cover the tracks that would allow us to spot authentic values. That is why the content of a work can by detestable: hateful or shocking, gratuitously violent or stripped of all humanity, and its form can enchant us through ingenious constructions and expressive techniques. Is such a work truly superior in essence? Does it ever reveal itself to be of the highest order? Does any criterion for establishing value prove to be impossible? And is the work we have done to define true beauty useless here?

The ancient Chinese did not resign themselves to such a stance, in any case. They understood that it was necessary to go beyond the level at which the various forms engendered by art appear, as well as the various tastes that humans exhibit; it was necessary to locate oneself resolutely on a higher level, further upstream, closer to the very source of Creation. As followers of the Tao, the Way, they were convinced that the course of the Way is itself continuous Creation, and that humans, through the act of creating, participate in it, and in this way earn their rank. Thus they attempted to extricate the ideas that define the necessary values based on the principle of life, ideas that are, let us repeat, in strict accord with their cosmology, according to which human gestures are bound to the "universal gestation."

⌒⌒⌒

Here, then, are the three fundamental notions that constitute a three-degree system. I will present them in the following organic order: *yin-yun, qi-yun,* and *shen-yun.*

1. First of all, at the very base, the first degree, is *yin-yun,* "unifying interaction." This notion signifies that the elements constituting a work must be engaged in a process of continual unifying interaction, a necessary condition for the work to become a living, organic unity. Taken literally, it evokes an atmospheric state, as when various elements, some related

to Yin, others to Yang, enter into contact, exchange. They attract one another, appeal to one another, interpenetrate one another to form a kind of magma, or rather an osmosis, from which the figures emerge and assert themselves, with their skeletal structure, flesh, form, and movement.

Metaphorically, the notion also suggests a sexual act in which the partners are aware of their difference even while tending toward union. All that is in the image of *Hun-dun,* "Initial Chaos," which contained the germ of such differentiation and which did not rest until the coming of Heaven and Earth was achieved. Once in place, those two each asserted their being, even while knowing that they were complements of each other, because they did not forget their original mixed state. Therein lies a perpetual dynamic movement of contrast and union that underlies the living matter of a pictorial work and is indispensable to it. With regard to Heaven-Earth, I think of the ideogram "one" that is written with a single horizontal stroke. In Chinese thought, this character represents the initial stroke—the primordial Breath—that separated Heaven and Earth; consequently it simultaneously signifies both division and unity.

Beginning from this character, how can we help but think of the theory of the single brushstroke dear to the great seventeenth-century painter Shitao? According to this theory, the single brushstroke, the basic unit, implicates all the possible and imaginable brushstrokes; it simultaneously embodies the one and the many, following the example of the primordial Breath, the basic unit that animates all beings. Possessing the single brushstroke, the artist can thus proceed to encounter the multiple, the immense, without ever losing himself; on the contrary, he is in a position to gain access to the higher order of unifying interaction. Moreover, Shitao devoted a chapter in his *Comments on Painting* to the idea of *yin-yun,* saying that, in a very concrete sense, the *yin-yun* also designates that decisive moment when the artist's brush encounters the ink to give birth to a figure or a scene. In the Chinese artistic imagination, the ink embodies all that is virtual in Nature in the process of coming to be, and the brush embodies the spirit of the artist who approaches and expresses this Nature waiting to be revealed. Thus, in the brush-ink that manifests the *yin-yun,* the carnal relationship between the feeling body of the artist and the felt body of the landscape is formed. In sum, the *yin-yun* is very much that intrinsic quality of a work: a unifying order rising from the very depths of an interaction on many levels between the various elements that constitute material, between the material and the spirit, and finally, between the human-subject and the living universe, itself a subject.

2. The intermediary degree is *qi-yun,* "rhythmic breath." "Let the rhythmic breath be animated" is one of the six rules for pictorial art established by Xie He at the beginning of the sixth century. The other rules concerned the study of the ancients, the principles of composition, the use of colors, and so on. This is the only one that touches on the soul of a work, in the sense that, from the author's perspective, the rhythmic breath is what structures a work at its depths and makes it radiate. This position was subsequently embraced by most

artists and "let the rhythmic breath be animated" became the "golden rule" of painting, and by extension, of calligraphy, poetry, and music. If the theme of rhythm occupies such an eminent place in Chinese art, it is because Chinese cosmology, based on the idea of the Breath, introduced, quite naturally, the theme of the great rhythm by which the living universe is supposedly animated.

Always in accordance with this cosmology, Chinese thought conceived that "the breath becomes the spirit when it achieves rhythm"; here, rhythm is almost synonymous with the internal law of living things that the Chinese call *li*. Let us quickly point out that the meaning of rhythm extends well beyond that of cadence, that insistent repetition of the same thing. In reality as in a work of art, the rhythm animates a given entity from within, but it is equally a matter of multiple entities in the presence of one another. It implies an intersection, an entanglement, even a clash when the work expresses rage or violence. Nevertheless, in a general way, rhythm aims at harmony in the dynamic sense of the word, a harmony made up of counterpoints and true repercussions. Its space-time is not at all one-dimensional. Following a spiral movement charged with restarts and rebounds, it always achieves a vertical intensity, engendering along the way unforeseen forms and unexpected echoes. It is in this sense that, within a work, the rhythmic breath is the unifier, structuring, merging, producing metamorphosis and transformation.

Since we are speaking of the Breath, this is a good opportunity to emphasize the importance of the Median Void, or rather the median voids. That is where the Breath is regenerated and circulates. These median voids, wide or narrow, obvious or hidden, give a work its respiration, punctuating the forms in it and allowing the unhoped-for to take place. I will allow myself to cite here some extracts from the brilliant text on rhythm by my teacher and friend Henri Maldiney, because it seems to me so relevant:

> The periodic return of the same, the principle of repetition that is cadence, is the absolute negation of that creation of unforeseeable, immovable novelty for which a rhythm is the event-advent. . . . All that, in the image of a wave. Its form in formation, with which we resonate, is the self-moving place of our encounter, always insistent with the world that envelopes us. Its ascent and descent do not succeed one another, they pass one another. At about the summit, while our expectation mounts, the ascending movement of the wave slows down, but before reaching its trough, it accelerates. Thus the two moments, ascending and descending, are each in precession, one with its opposite. They could not be freed of one another, without losing, along with their coexistence, the dimension according to which they exist. The moments of a rhythm exist only in reciprocity, in its unforeseeable advent. . . . A rhythm does not unfold in time and space, it is the generator of its space-time. The advent of a rhythmic space only happens with the constituent transformation of all the elements of a work of art in moment of form, in moment of rhythm. This rhythm cannot be had beforehand; it is

not of the order of having. We *are* in rhythm. Present to it, we discover ourselves present to ourselves. We exist in this opening in existence. Rhythm is a form of existence surprised. . . . Rare are the works in the presence of which we have the grounds for *being*. The nave of Sainte-Sophie of Constantinople, Mouki's "Persimmons," Cézanne's Sainte-Victoire in the Saint Petersburg museum . . .[7]

3. Finally, the highest degree, *shen-yun*, "divine resonance." This expression designates the supreme quality that a work must possess to be of primary greatness. It is hard to grasp this because it really seems to suggest something abstract and vague. The Chinese are wary of too rigidly defining it, considering the quality that it evokes is a state that "one is in a position to feel without being able to explain."

Let us nevertheless try to define it as precisely as possible. *Shen* embodies the superior state of *qi*, "Breath": it is generally translated as the spirit or the divine spirit. Just like *qi*, *shen* is at the foundation of the living universe. Whereas, according to Chinese thought, the primordial Breath animates all forms of life, the Spirit, for its part, governs the mental part, the conscious part of the living universe. This conception can be astonishing. To say that man, as a thinking being, is inhabited by *shen* seems acceptable to everyone. But on the other hand, to affirm that the universe itself is inhabited by *shen* as well, and that, most importantly, it is governed by it, can appear suspect to a pure materialist. The deep reason for such a conception is that Chinese thought does not separate matter and spirit. It reasons in terms of *life*, which is the basic unit. It distinguishes levels in the order of life but does not recognize discontinuities, organic ruptures between them. Many consider the people shaped by this thinking to be "unreligious," and that is probably true. That did not prevent Buddhism, Islam, and Christianity from subsequently taking root in China. But, in their way, the Chinese had a sense of the sacred, a sacred that is none other than that of the Way, that irresistible progress of open life. One sentence, apparently naive owing to its simplicity, seems to define it, a sentence contained in the commentaries on *The Book of Changes:* "Life engenders Life, there will be no end."

Here, life takes on a meaning that surpasses the simple fact of existence: it signifies all that life always contains as promise. It is this inalienable, open principle that bears the name of divine spirit. How does the sacred, this *shen,* that inhabits the living universe just as it does mankind, bear responsibility for the suffering born of the mortal condition? By its exigency and impartiality, it can seem "indifferent;" and humans, often crushed by fear, suffering, or hatred, can demand explanation or do it violence. But the sacred itself is not violence.

With artists, *shen* maintains a relationship of collaboration. The greatest among them, poets and painters alike, have claimed that their brushes were "guided by *shen*." Let us remember that the literati tradition, which assigned poetry and painting to the highest place among human accomplishments, hardly distinguishes the aesthetic from the ethical. It exhorts the artist to practice saintliness if he wants his own spirit to encounter the divine spirit at the highest level. The

Chinese language has the habit of associating *shen*, "divine spirit," and *sheng*, "saintliness." And the compound word *shen-sheng*, "divine spirit-saintliness," exists, precisely, to designate that privileged moment when the human *sheng* enters into dialogue with the universal *shen* that opens to him the most secret, intimate part of the living universe, in such a way that the expression "divine resonance" is to be understood in the sense of "in resonance with the divine spirit." This idea is thus essentially musical; musicality is, in fact, essential to Chinese art. Nevertheless, as it concerns painting and poetry, the visual aspect cannot be neglected; to understand the notion of "divine resonance," we must appeal to the idea of vision and to that of presence.

In a painting, the landscape that the artist produces with his or her brush can be lofty or tempestuous, dense or ethereal, suffused with light or permeated with mystery. The important thing is that this landscape goes beyond the dimensions of representation alone, and that it offers itself as a vision, an advent: the advent of a presence—not in the figurative or anthropological sense of the word—that can be felt or sensed, the very presence of the divine spirit. With all its share of the invisible, this presence corresponds to what the Chinese theoreticians call the *xiang-wai-zhi-xiang*, "image beyond images." It is also close to what *Chan* spirituality experiences as illumination: as, before a natural scene, a tree in blossom, a bird calling as it takes flight, a ray of sun or moonlight that illuminates a moment of silence, one suddenly passes to the other side of the scene. Thus one finds oneself beyond the screen of phenomena, experiencing the impression of a presence that is self-generating, that comes to us whole, indivisible, inexplicable, and nevertheless undeniable, such a generous gift that makes all that exists *there,* miraculously *there,* emanating a light of the original hue, whispering a native song from heart to heart, from soul to soul.

I have just used the word *soul.* It evokes for me the notion of *yi-jing,* "dimension of the soul," which we have already encountered in the second meditation with regard to the rose, and which, in Chinese aesthetic thought, is almost equivalent to our *shen-yun,* "divine resonance." Just like *shen, yi,* "disposition of the heart, the soul," is that with which both man and the living universe are endowed. The *yi-jing* thus suggests a soul-to-soul collaboration between the human and the divine, which the Chinese language designates by the expression *mo-qi,* "tacit understanding." An understanding that is never complete: there will always be a hiatus, a suspension, a failure to fulfill. The desired infinite is very much that, un-finite, unfinished. The void that fills the scroll of a Chinese painting is there to represent it. The void moved by the Breath harbors a waiting, a listening that is ready to welcome a new advent, herald a new understanding. In view of this, the artist, for his part, is always ready to endure grief and suffering, loss and deprivation, to the point of letting himself be consumed by the fire of his action, letting himself be inhaled by the space of the work. He knows that beauty, more than a given, is the supreme gift of whatever has been offered. And for man, more than an acquisition, it will always be a challenge, a wager.

NOTES

FIRST MEDITATION

1. Fyodor Dostoyevsky, *L'Idiot* (Paris: Gallimard, Folio Collection, 2001), part 3, ch. 1.
2. Henri Maldiney, *Ouvrir le rien. L'art nu* (La Versanne, France: Encre Marine, 2000).

SECOND MEDITATION

1. Alain Michel, *La Parole et la Beauté: Rhétorique et esthétique dans la tradition occidentale* (Paris: Albin Michel, 1982, 1994), 48.
2. Angelus Silesius, *Le Pèlerin chérubinique* (Paris: Le Cerf, 1994), book 1, sec. 289, p. 97.
3. Lao-tzu, *Tao Te Ching* (Paris: Albin Michel, Spiritualités vivant poche Collection, 1984), sec. 1.
4. Paul Claudel, *L'Oiseau noir dans le soleil levant,* in *Connaisance de l'Est* (Paris: Gallimard, Poésie Collection, 2000), 291.
5. Paul Claudel, "La Cantate à trois voix," in *Cinq Grandes Odes* (Paris: Gallimard, Poésie Collection, 1966), 137.

6. Charles Baudelaire, "Élévation," in *Les Fleurs du mal* (Paris: Le Livre de poche, 1972).

7. Lao-tzu, *Tao Te Ching*, sec. 33.

8. John Keats, *Endymion: A Poetic Romance,* book 1, vol. 1, in *The Poetical Works of John Keats* (London: n.p., 1884).

THIRD MEDITATION

1. François Dolbeau, "Sermon inédit de saint Augustin sur la providence divine," in *Revue des études augustiniennes* XLI (1995): 283.

2. Michelangelo, *Sonnets* (Paris: Club français du livre, 1961).

3. Paul Verlaine, "Clair du lune," in *Fêtes galantes,* 1869.

4. France Quéré, *Le Sel et le Vent* (Paris: Bayard, 1995), 150–52.

5. Rainer Maria Rilke, "Sonnets à Orphée," I, 3, in *Les Élégies du Duino, Les Sonnets à Orphée* (Paris: Le Seuil, Points-poésie Collection, 2006).

6. Le Siracide (L'Ecclésiastique), XXXII, 5.

7. Henri Bergson, *La Pensée et le Mouvant: Essais et conférences* (Paris: Presses universitaire de France, Quadrige-Grands textes Collection, 2003), 280.

8. Plotinus, "Traité 38: Comment la multiplicité des idées s'est établie et sur le Bien," in *Traités 38–41* (Paris: Garnier-Flammarion, 2007).

9. Ibid, 78.

10. Emerich Kastner, ed., *Ludwig van Beethovens sämtliche Briefe* [Complete Correspondance of Ludwig van Beethoven] (Leipzig: n.p., 1923), 224.

FOURTH MEDITATION

1. Nicolas Boileau, "Epistre IX," in *Oeuvres complètes* (Paris: Gallimard, la Pléiade Collection, 1966), 134.

2. Alfred de Musset, *Premières Poésies—Poésies nouvelles* (Paris: Gallimard, Poésie collection, 1976), 386.

3. Grant F. Scott, ed., *Selected Letters of John Keats* (Cambridge and London: Harvard University Press, 2002), 290.

4. John Keats, "Ode on a Grecian Urn," in *Les Odes* (Paris: Arfuyen, 1996).

5. Friedrich Hölderlin, "En bleu adorable . . . ," in *Poèmes de Hölderlin traduit par André du Bouchet* (Paris: Mercure de France, 1963), 44.

6. *Les Entretiens de Confucius* (Paris: Gallimard, Folio collection, 2005), VI, 23, p. 37, and IX, 28, p. 54.

7. Henri Maldiney, *L'Avènement de l'oeuvre* (Saint-Maximin, France: Théétète, 1997).

8. Meister Eckhart, *Sur la naissance de Dieu dans l'âme, Sermons 101–104* (Paris: Arfuyen, 2004).

9. Julien Green, *Oeuvres complètes* (Paris: Gallimard, la Pléiade Collection, 1977), vol. V, p. 924.

10. Angelus Silesius, *Le Pèlerin chérubinique,* book 1, sec. 8, p. 34.

FIFTH MEDITATION

1. Max Jacob, *L'Homme de cristal: Poèmes* (Paris: Gallimard, 1967), 45.

2. Max Jacob, *Derniers Poèmes en vers et en prose* (Paris: Gallimard, 1961), 118.

3. Baudelaire, "Les Phares," in *Les Fleurs du mal.*

4 Plato, *Phaedrus* (Paris: Garnier-Flammarion, 2006), 124.

5. Aristotle, *Metaphysics* (Paris: Garnier-Flammarion, 2008), book M, 4, p. 1078a.

6. Emmanuel Kant, *Critique de la faculté de juger* (Paris: Gallimard, Folio essais Collection, 1985), 139, 152, 175.

7. Henri Maldiney, "Notes sur le rythme," in *Fario,* no. 1 (2005).

BOOKS OF RELATED INTEREST

The Meditator's Guidebook
Pathways to Greater Awareness and Creativity
by Lucy Oliver

Meditations on the Peaks
Mountain Climbing as Metaphor for the Spiritual Quest
by Julius Evola

Nine Designs for Inner Peace
The Ultimate Guide to Meditating with Color, Shape, and Sound
by Sarah Tomlinson

The Science of Happiness
10 Principles for Manifesting Your Divine Nature
by Ryuho Okawa

The Law of Attention
Nada Yoga and the Way of Inner Vigilance
by Edward Salim Michael

Fusion of the Five Elements
Meditations for Transforming Negative Emotions
by Mantak Chia

Living in the Tao
The Effortless Path of Self-Discovery
by Mantak Chia and William U. Wei

The Practice of Tibetan Meditation
Exercises, Visualizations, and Mantras for Health and Well-being
by Dagsay Tulku Rinpoche

Inner Traditions • Bear & Company
P.O. Box 388
Rochester, VT 05767
1-800-246-8648
www.InnerTraditions.com

Or contact your local bookseller